The Kings' Mistresses

For Betty

The Kings'Mistresses

Alan Hardy

Evans Brothers Limited London

Published by Evans Brothers Limited
Montague House, Russell Square
London, WC1B 5BX

Set in 11 on 12pt Plantin by
Filmtype Services Limited, Scarborough
Printed and bound in Great Britain by
Redwood Burn Limited
Trowbridge & Esher

Hardy, Alan
    The Kings' Mistresses.
    1. Mistresses – Great Britain
    2. Favorites, Royal – Great Britain
    2. Great Britain – Kings and rulers
    I. Title
    941'.00992   DA308

ISBN 0–237–45526–9
PRA 7105

Contents

Introduction	Many strange women	9
Charles II	A little pleasure out of the way	11
Charles II	Where the deer laid	30
James II	The forbidden love of women	41
William III	But one vice	53
George I	So uncommon a seraglio	64
George II	The right sow by the ear	78
George IV	Ye pleasures of Elyssium	95
George IV	A colt out to grass	106
William IV	Those damned women	118
Edward VII	Yielding to temptation	132
Edward VII	Sinning as with a cart-rope	143
Edward VIII	The tide of his ardour	156
Edward VIII	Make Mrs Simpson his mistress	164

Sources	176
Select Bibliography	182
Index	184

List of Illustrations

Between pages 72 and 73
Charles II by Samuel Cooper (The Mansell Collection)
Lucy Walter, after a miniature in the Buccleuch Collection
(BBC Hulton Picture Library)
James, Duke of Monmouth (BBC Hulton Picture Library)
Catherine of Braganza (BBC Hulton Picture Library)
Nell Gwyn, from an original by Lely (BBC Hulton Picture
Library)
Louise de Keroualle (Mary Evans Picture Library)
Barbara Villiers, Duchess of Cleveland (Mary Evans Picture
Library)
Anne Hyde, Duchess of York, after Lely (BBC Hulton
Picture Library)
Lady Denham (BBC Hulton Picture Library)
James II by Samuel Cooper (BBC Hulton Picture Library)
Catherine Sedley, Countess of Dorchester (Mary Evans
Picture Library)
Ehrengarde, Duchess of Kendal (BBC Hulton Picture
Library)
George I, after Ravenet (BBC Hulton Picture Library)
'Solomon in his glory' – anonymous cartoon showing George
II and Madame Walmoden (reproduced by Courtesy of the
Trustees of the British Museum)
Caroline of Anspach, wife of George II (Mansell Collection)

Between pages 136 and 137
Cartoon of George IV by Cruikshank, from 'The Queen's
Matrimonial Ladder' (1820) (Mary Evans Picture Library)
George IV (The Mansell Collection)
Caroline of Brunswick, wife of George IV (BBC Hulton
Picture Library)
'Bergami's Little Darling' (Mansell Collection)
Locket containing a portrait of Mrs Fitzherbert by Richard
Cosway (reproduced by permission of the Trustees, The
Wallace Collection, London)
'Wife and No Wife or A Trip to the Continent' by Gillray
(1788) (BBC Hulton Picture Library)

'A King-Fisher' (Mansell Collection)

Frances Countess of Jersey, after D. Gardiner (BBC Hulton Picture Library)

Isabella, Marchioness of Hertford (BBC Hulton Picture Library)

Dorothea Jordan by George Romney (BBC Hulton Picture Library)

'Royal Navy' by George Cruikshank (Mansell Collection)

Queen Alexandra in 1905 (BBC Hulton Picture Library)

Edward VII by G. F. Watts (National Portrait Gallery, London)

Lily Langtry by Millais (BBC Hulton Picture Library)

Frances, Countess of Warwick (BBC Hulton Picture Library)

Alice Keppel, from a drawing by Ellis Roberts (BBC Hulton Picture Library)

Mrs Simpson, a photograph from the French magazine *L'Illustration* (Mansell Collection)

Thelma, Viscountess Furness (BBC Hulton Picture Library)

Introduction

Many Strange Women

It was not King Solomon alone who, as the Book of Kings has it, 'loved many strange women'. The role of mistress to the monarch has existed as long as the institution of monarchy itself, and for reasons that are understandable enough. Kings throughout history have, more often than not, been subject to an abnormal upbringing, in all probability obliged to enter loveless marriages for reasons of state, starved of normal family life and ordained to live perpetually surrounded by courtiers and attendants, circumscribed by pomp and etiquette.

To have a mistress was to beat the system, and in consequence few monarchs have been either celibate or monogamous. Most have been eager to rush into the arms of women who attracted them, not only as a means of fulfilling their carnal desires but – often just as important – in order to enjoy a relaxed informal relationship away from duty and ceremony. Sometimes these relationships turned out to be the briefest of casual affairs, at other times they blossomed into a lifetime of devotion.

Such liaisons were unlikely to remain unknown for long. As one seventeenth-century observer put it, 'Though Princes be as secret as they will in such matters they are always known'. Even so, whatever the moral climate of the age, there was never any shortage of candidates to share the royal bed, to whisper on the royal pillow – and in the process, like as not, to use their charms as a means of furthering their own ambitions. The clever ones had more than one way of holding their lover in thrall. As physical passion tended to die down, a soothing manner, conversational ability and a faculty to amuse were useful devices for perpetuating a prestigious royal attachment.

For the stakes were high, since kingship is concerned with power, sometimes absolute power. And even in Britain, where over the last three hundred years royal authority has been reduced from near autocracy to little more than the right to be told what is going to happen, still the institution has retained some political leverage, together with considerable wealth and enormous social prestige.

This book sets out to follow, not only the follies and idiosyncracies of individual monarchs, but also the varying degrees to which their female favourites have affected the life of the country during those three centuries. Though it is often difficult to be precise, since royal pillow talk rarely gets further than the bedroom door, there is more than enough evidence to show that royal mistresses were a force to be reckoned with in affairs of state. In some cases the political influence some were thought to exercise turns out to have been exaggerated – but the importance of others has not always been sufficiently appreciated.

Of course it was often the case in the past, as it is today, that it was not the truth that was important in influencing events, but what people believed to be the truth, something which has a particular relevance to the usually clandestine activities of this shadowy profession. And certainly the monarch's extra-marital activities, together with his mistress's low standing in public esteem, have frequently had a significant effect on a particular king's popularity and have indeed sometimes sapped the very foundations of the monarchy.

The kings' mistresses therefore were not merely pretty faces or heavenly bodies. Their existence and their activities, as the following pages set out to demonstrate, are woven deep into the fabric of Britain's political and social history. I have attempted to unravel some of the threads.

Charles II
A Little Pleasure Out Of The Way

One day in July in the year 1648 a young man eighteen years of age quietly left his mother in Paris and made his way to the Dutch coast to meet his younger brother. This journey of seeming insignificance took place against a background of high drama. The young man was Charles, Prince of Wales. He met his brother James at the port of Helvoetsluys where part of the English navy was at anchor. The men in these ships had revolted against the English Parliament and it was young Charles's hope that their defection would enable him to assist his father, King Charles I, who was held at this time as a prisoner by Parliament. The young man's lack of success was underlined by an act which took place six months later. On a cold January morning Charles I, with enviable equanimity, stepped on to a platform outside the Banqueting House in Whitehall and had his head severed from his body, an event hallowed by Andrew Marvell in the famous words, 'He nothing common did nor mean upon that memorable scene'.

Whether Charles I 'nothing common did nor mean' in the political field is a subject on which historians have grave doubts. What is unarguable is that in his private life he had been a faithful and loving husband to Queen Henrietta Maria and a dutiful father to his children. Unfortunately family life had been shattered by the Civil War, an interruption which had a profound effect on the lives of those children and not least on his eldest sons who were to become Charles II and James II.

11

Charles II reckoned his reign began the instant his father's head left his body. Not yet nineteen, he had already been in exile for some years. His formidable mother, a French princess who had once more made her home in France, did her best to govern him but, young though he was, he refused to be governed. His father had been the most uxorious of men and, almost as if to prove that he was not going to subject himself to the same control, this Charles began the practice of falling into the arms of as many beautiful women as attracted him. Against the background of his shattered existence sexual waywardness is at least understandable, even if Charles overcompensated. Away from the spirit of puritan England he absorbed the moral laxity of France. His inspiration, if he needed one, was his maternal grandfather Henri IV of France.

There had been speculation that young Charles had been initiated in the mysteries of the fair sex before he left England. His first such proven experience to produce a permanent result occurred during that otherwise unsuccessful visit to Helvoetsluys. He arrived there on 9 July, and exactly nine months later his son was born. The mother was a young Welsh girl of good family named Lucy Walter. She had already been living with another man and, to give herself some status, now called herself Mrs Barlow. To John Evelyn, the diarist, who met her at this time she was 'this beautiful strumpet ... a brown, beautiful, bold, but insipid creature'.

The son she bore, Evelyn thought, was too good-looking to be Charles's. ('Seldom was he possessed of their first favours', a contemporary was to suggest of Charles's mistresses.) But Charles II's own heavy dark looks were quite capable of producing handsome offspring, especially when crossed with beautiful women, as his later affairs were to prove. He had no hesitation in recognising this child, the future Duke of Monmouth, as his own, and he was to lavish much love and attention on the boy, to be repaid in due time with much trouble.

As for Lucy Walter, she lived up to her reputation as a beautiful strumpet, bequeathing her favours elsewhere during her royal lover's temporary absence in England at the time of the Battle of Worcester. As far as Charles was concerned this cancelled out any claims she had on him. She died a few years later – of a disease incident on her profession, according to James II's autobiography; 'miserably,' according to Evelyn, 'without anything to bury her'. Meanwhile Charles had gained possession of the child.

Throughout his twenties Charles II remained a king without a throne, wandering with a threadbare court from country to country. His prospects were poor and he was nearly always short of money, though rarely without feminine consolation. At this stage in his life marriage offered no channel for his urges. His lack of prospects made him a less than eligible match for a bride of proper status, and as he had little to look forward to, but plenty of time on his hands, casual affairs provided an easy diversion. Says Gilbert Burnet, the future Bishop of Salisbury: 'During his exile he delivered himself so entirely to his pleasures that he became incapable of application.' He also became completely amoral – he was to tell Burnet 'he could not think God would make a man miserable, only for taking a little pleasure out of the way'. From the time he was twenty till he was thirty he went from one woman to the next, something which many Royalists felt did his cause no good. He is reputed to have had seventeen mistresses before his restoration to the throne. Among them was Elizabeth Killigrew, daughter of Sir William Killigrew who had been in his father's service, by whom he had a daughter; and the beautiful Catherine Pegge, daughter of a Derbyshire squire, who produced for him another son, later created Earl of Plymouth. Till he met Barbara Palmer, just before his return home, these love affairs reflected his life: restless, for ever on the move, taking his pleasure where he could.

He first met Barbara Palmer, to be described as 'the lewdest as well as the fairest of King Charles's concubines', when he was twenty-nine and she ten years younger. Like most of his previous mistresses she came from a good background of country gentry. Her family life, like his, had been marred by war. Like him, too, she had been attracted early to affairs of the heart. Burnet was to sum her up, not unfairly, as 'most enormously vicious and ravenous; foolish but imperious, very uneasy to the King, and always carrying on intrigues with other men'. Her mother had read her well and married her off when she was eighteen to another Royalist, Roger Palmer. But this loveless marriage did nothing to stop Barbara from pursuing the affair she had previously been having with the amorous young Earl of Chesterfield. This was still going on when she was selected to go on a Royalist mission to Charles at Breda. There her good looks and auburn hair made her a success in more ways than her relatives had bargained for. She had a beauty and a sensuality which was to tie him to her longer than anyone he had previously met, and this in spite of her more aggressive qualities, which in bed may have had their attractions but which in public could be degrading.

Other negotiations in Breda had more important repercussions, with the result that in May 1660, on his thirtieth birthday, Charles II made his triumphant return home to his throne. Tradition has it that he spent his first night in London in the arms of Barbara Palmer. At any rate, it was nine months after his return that their first child, later created Countess of Sussex, was born. It was not long before it was apparent to those of his subjects in the know that this King Charles was as easy-going in his morals as his father had been strait-laced. Whatever might be accepted practice in the France of young Louis XIV, in England no king had kept a mistress since Henry VIII, and even he had fallen into the habit of marrying the women he coveted. Not that there could be much question of Charles II marrying for love. In the century or more which had elapsed since Henry VIII's death the importance of dynastic marriages had grown, so it was obvious that this king, on a still unstable throne, must, like his father and grandfather, make a suitable marriage with a foreign princess.

While a dynastic arrangement was being negotiated the mistress held unchallenged sway. At first this involved meetings at the Palmers' house in King Street, just outside the Palace of Whitehall. To mollify the cuckolded husband (and at the same time give his mistress a title), Charles created Roger Palmer Earl of Castlemaine – with succession to the title limited to Barbara's children. After the arrival of another child, however, Lord Castlemaine finally separated from his wayward spouse. But, as if to spite her, he survived for another forty years, so preventing her from remarrying till she was an old woman.

By the time Lady Castlemaine's second child, the future Duke of Southampton, was expected Charles's own position was complicated by the fact that it had been agreed he should marry the Portugese Infanta, Catherine of Braganza. Her arrival in England appeared to give him an opportunity to regularise the position of his by now heavily pregnant mistress. With little feeling for the susceptibilities of his bride he accordingly included Barbara's name among the Ladies of the Bedchamber. To his surprise Catherine struck out the name and refused to reinstate it. The Lord Chancellor, the Earl of Clarendon, who, as Edward Hyde, had been the King's most faithful supporter in exile, was in an unenviable position. In general he saw it as part of his duty to protect his master from what he called 'the torrent of his impetuous passions'. In particular he disapproved of Charles's relations with Lady Castlemaine and did not mince his words. England, he pointed out, was not France where 'such friendships are not new in the Court nor scandalous in the Kingdom'. In England if a women prostituted herself even to the King she was regarded as being no better than a common whore, as Anne Boleyn had discovered. And at least the mistresses of the French kings were 'women of great quality, and who had never been tainted by any other familiarity'. It took courage for Clarendon to stick to this line for at this stage in constitutional development ministers retained office only during the monarch's pleasure.

Over Barbara's position in the Queen's entourage Charles remained adamant. 'I am resolved to go through with this matter, let what will come of it,' he stubbornly declared, 'and whosoever I find to be my Lady Castlemaine's enemy in this matter, I do promise on my word to be his enemy as long as I live'. 'I have undone this lady,' he reasoned with more loyalty than accuracy, 'and ruined her reputation, which was fair and untainted till her friendship with me, and I am obliged in conscience and honour to repair her to the utmost in my power.' He was not prepared to give up seeing her, maintaining somewhat ambiguously, 'I like her company and conversation, from which I will not be restrained, because I know there is and will be all innocence in it'. He did make this promise: 'My wife shall never have cause to complain that I broke my vows to her if she will live towards me as a good wife ought to do.' From this it would appear he had formed a resolution of being faithful to the marriage bed. Apparently with the idea that an official post at court would be sufficient recompense to

Lady Castlemaine for ending their relationship, he confirmed to Clarendon 'I will contain myself within the strict bounds of virtue'.

Having first introduced his mistress into his wife's presence by stealth, Charles had his way over the appointment, and Lady Castlemaine was set up in her own apartment in the Palace of Whitehall. The new Queen, after initial heart-searching and an occasional recurrence of irritation, found the most rewarding way to conduct herself was to be as affectionate and tolerant as possible. In return Charles was kind, courteous and grateful – though his gratitude stopped short of fidelity. Any good intentions he had in that direction did not survive for long. As was often the case when marital hopes had been based on flattering miniatures and descriptions by third parties, Catherine – short of stature, of sallow complexion, with protruding teeth – did not live up to expectations. As Henry VIII had been dissatisfied with his 'Flanders mare', Anne of Cleves, Charles found little to attract him physically to Catherine of Braganza, though for a time he did try to do his duty.

For some years he made a practice of spending the evening with his mistress but then returning to the marital bed for the rest of the night, and on one occasion he even wrote to his sister 'I have been all this afternoon playing the good husband and I am very sleepy'. It was not his fault that his wife failed to produce a child. There were early hopes, but after two miscarriages never afterwards much optimism. Even so, to his credit, he would never contemplate divorce. The fact that his wife learned to accept his numerous liaisons with quiet dignity meant that Charles could not, in all conscience, contemplate getting rid of her even under pressure to secure the succession to the throne. 'I will not suffer an innocent woman to be wronged.' In later years Catherine lived largely at Somerset House, a sort of premature dower house, leaving her husband even more free to follow his inclinations.

The absence of a legitimate child, leaving the King's brother James as heir, weakened the position of Clarendon as architect of the marriage. In the longer term it was to have disastrous consequences for the future of the Stuart dynasty and the country. The barrenness of Queen Catherine was in tremendous contrast to the King's fruitful liaisons elsewhere.

If one excludes Lady Castlemaine's last child, whose paternity is in doubt, Charles II is known to have fathered thirteen bastards. The fact that Lady Castlemaine presented him with a child in each of the three years after his marriage is indication enough of how unfulfilled were any resolutions he may have made when he married.

Lady Castlemaine, with her expensive tastes and her greed, also made other more material acquisitions. With her appetite for money constantly being sharpened she was soon mistress of the arts of wheedling, bribery and corruption. The generous Charles was easy prey, gratifying among other things her delight in jewellery. When Evelyn saw mistress and queen together the mistress was decked in jewellery 'esteemed at 40,000 pounds or more and far outshining the Queen'. When insatiable Barbara did not get jewels in sufficient quantity from her lover she bought them herself, and when she could not pay the bill she presented it to him.

In addition to the occasional settling of her debts (Pepys reported one such settlement of £30,000) regular provision was made for her out of funds at the King's disposal. As well as outright grants of money from his privy purse, rents from land he gave her, and Queen Elizabeth's favourite Palace of Nonsuch which she sold for demolition, there was the £10,000 or so a year she obtained from the excise on beer, £5,500 from wine licences and £5,000 from the Post Office. All in all, it can be reckoned that a considerable portion of the funds and estates at the King's disposal at the time of his restoration were handed over to support the extravagance of this and other mistresses, as well as to finance his bastards – one reason why he was always chronically short of money.

Then there was bribery, at which Lady Castlemaine became increasingly adept. Very often this took the form of accepting money from office-seekers, who used her to secure for them jobs in the royal gift. Such jobs having been obtained, it was then customary for a second thank-you present to be made. Foreign ambassadors were often willing to give a handsome bribe if the mistress would put in a sympathetic word for them and their causes. In Lady Castlemaine's case what she received went like water through a sieve. For in addition to her extravagant mode of living, fine clothes, the jewels and the costly apartments, she became a great gambler, her passion for games of chance not being matched by any great ability to win. 'I was told tonight,' wrote Samuel Pepys in 1668, 'that my Lady Castlemaine is so great a gambler as to have won £15,000 in one night, and lost £25,000 in another night, at play, and hath played £1,000 and £1,500 at a cast.' 'His Majesty,' runs another report, 'gave the Commissioners of the Treasury fair warning to look after themselves, for that she would have a bout with them for money, having lately lost £20,000 in money and jewels in one night at play.' Charles might make light of such wild spending, financed in the end by himself, but many who had suffered great financial loss for their loyalty to the throne and then went unrewarded were deeply offended by such waste.

In the early years Lady Castlemaine's acquisitiveness was curbed by the actions of the powerful Clarendon to whom, as Evelyn picturesquely put it, she was 'an eye sore'. Disapproving as he did of the whole business, Claredon blocked any attempted gift to her out of official sources. Not surprisingly she came to regard him as her greatest enemy, and as she became more closely involved with the court and its politics it became her prime object to get rid of him. In this she found ready allies among younger politicians on the make, and her evening parties became well-known for attracting the ambitious. Clarendon himself considered her 'weak and easily managed', easy prey for those wishing to make use of her. But such alliances could be mutually beneficial. Pepys was convinced that the future Lord Arlington, for one, owed much of his advancement to her influence. When, seven years after the restoration, Clarendon fell, as he left his last audience the old man observed Lady Castlemaine and Arlington laughing at his departure. Charles's action in getting rid of him cannot, however, be explained merely as the victory of his mistress. For some years he had been tiring of Clarendon, his sermonising and the power he sought to exercise over him. Therefore when he judged the time right, he dropped him.

It is unlikely that any mistress ever persuaded so wily and cynical a man as Charles II to do anything of importance that was not already in his mind. This was not generally realised. Among observers, Lady Castlemaine's influence was thought to count for a great deal, and much effort was wasted on discussions as to how far she was in favour with her lover at a particular time. After Clarendon's time, ministers tended to feel so unsure of themselves and so mistrustful of one another that they were only too anxious to use whatever channels were available to obtain royal favour. So Lady Castlemaine, in Burnet's words, 'held a sort of court' in her apartments where Charles was apt to call on her, and where 'all his ministers made application to them'.

In the same way the suspected influence of Charles II's mistresses, and particularly the two who were in effect *maîtresses en titre* for almost the whole of his reign, coloured the King's relations with the House of Commons. That the mistresses had an apparently insatiable appetite for money, and that the King was slave enough to seek to satisfy them, was widely suspected. Members of Parliament, though they did not know the size of the bill, had a shrewd idea it was a big one. During this reign the relative strengths of King and Parliament were being put to the test, with a certain amount of brinkmanship on both sides. It was also a time of almost perpetual shortage of money for the King's needs, and rumours of the extravagance of his mistresses were no help to him when it came to selling his cause to a tight-fisted Parliament. As the reign progressed Charles's foreign policies came under increasing suspicion, and there was in any case a feeling that except in time of war a monarch ought to be able to live on his hereditary income. All this led not only to an increasingly critical view of the King and his financial needs but also to an attempt of far-reaching constitutional significance to control more tightly the supply of money and its allocation.

How far the King's preoccupation with women affected his capacity to rule has long been the subject of conjecture. It certainly worried many people at the time. Gilbert Burnet was one who shook his head over the effect on the King of the temperamental Lady Castlemaine. 'His passion for her and her strange behaviour did so disorder him that he was not master over himself or his business.' 'The King,' it was suggested another time, 'hath taken ten times more time at making friends between Lady Castlemaine and Mrs Stuart, when they have fallen out than ever he did to save his kingdom.' Samuel Pepys, early in the reign, had been smitten by Castlemaine's looks, 'tho' I know she is a whore', and when he saw her petticoats hanging out to dry he admitted 'it did me good to look upon them'. Later he came to agree with his friend Sir Thomas Crew 'that the King minds nothing but pleasures, and hates the very sight or thought of business; that my Lady Castlemaine rules him who, he says, hath all the tricks of Aretin that are to be practised to give pleasure'.

It is true that without his emotional entanglements and the histrionics of his lady friends, Charles would have had much more time at his disposal. With such distractions he became, for instance, far from regular in attending meetings of his Council. As Anthony Hamilton explained: 'He shewed great abilities in urgent affairs, but was incapable of application to any that were not so.' But, given his nature, it is doubtful whether he would have attended to his business more diligently had he been satisfied with his queen. It was his way to take firm measures only when circumstances forced him to do so: normally to affect indifference but to be ready to pounce when required. With his lethargy and his escapist disposition, had he not been so fond of the fair sex he might well have resorted to heavier drinking and gambling for diversion – with worse consequences than womanising brought him.

Still, this was a time when puritan standards were still fresh in the minds of older people, especially, and even among many disposed to be loyal to the restored monarchy. John Evelyn, whose attachment to the throne was matched by his own high moral standards, was convinced that for Charles to consort with 'prostitute creatures' did his cause infinite harm. 'An excellent prince doubtless,' he was to write when the King died, 'had he been less addicted to women, which made him uneasy and always in want to supply their immeasurable profusion, and to the detriment of many indigent persons who had signally served both him and his father.' It was bad enough that for male company the new King gravitated towards young bloods, whose behaviour tended to cause public scandal. But the whole atmosphere of the court was pervaded at best by frivolity, and at worst decadence, so that for instance, as Anthony Hamilton pointed out, 'Lady Middleton, Lady Denham, the queen's and the duchess's maids of honour, and a hundred others bestow their favours to the right and to the left, and not the least notice is taken of their conduct'. Why should any notice have been taken, when the monarch himself was not prepared to exercise the slightest discretion with regard to his mistresses or his illegitimate offspring? His attitude was consistent throughout. At the beginning of his reign it shocked his subjects to see their new King riding in a coach with his mother, his mistress and his eldest bastard. Later, Burnet noted, 'he usually came from his mistress's lodgings to church, even on sacrament days'; and it set tongues wagging when he was seen to attend divine service on Easter Day later on in life accompanied by three of his natural sons.

Charles II appears indeed to have had an inner compulsion to give the seal of respectability and official recognition both to his mistresses and their offspring. None of his children was legitimised, as he well knew that this would endanger the succession to the throne, but their royal paternity was fully recognised. It was Charles's love for his handsome and engaging son by Lucy Walter which set him on this road. Thereafter titles were usually forthcoming for his sons, sometimes with official positions and emoluments, and good marriages were arranged as early as possible. The girls too were provided with husbands, preferably monied and titled.

When Charles made known his wish to raise up his eldest son, he was strongly opposed by Clarendon. All objections were pushed aside however, the boy was recognised as his natural son and created Duke of Monmouth. Accepting the offer of the mother of the extremely rich twelve-year-old Countess of Buccleuch, the King married him off at the age of fourteen, granting him pensions to keep him in an appropriate state independent of his wife. £8,000 a year was granted to him from the export of white draperies, £6,000 from excise receipts and a proportion of the money due to the Crown from prizes and wrecks. As Master of the Horse, with high command in the army, and, at his father's suggestion, Chancellor of Cambridge University, this son could never complain that his father had not looked after him. Spoilt and susceptible to flattery, he soon was following his father's example with mistresses and illegitimate offspring of his own. And before long greater cause for anxiety began to loom on the horizon.

Among the King's other natural children the Dukes of Southampton and Grafton, both sons of Lady Castlemaine, were engaged to heiresses when they were only nine years old.

Grafton, who was to grow into the handsomest of Charles's handsome sons, was married at the age of twelve to his child fiancée, the only daughter and heiress of Lord Arlington. As her mother made clear, 'the King would have it so'. Normally parents, rich and noble though they might be, were only too happy to co-operate in such ventures. So it was that Charles's ambitious minister, Danby, married his daughter to the Earl of Plymouth; and the Duke of Norfolk boasted to Evelyn of planning to marry his son to one of the King's daughters 'by which he reckoned he shall come into mighty favour'.

Most people, with nothing to gain, took a very different view of the King's private affairs. Pepys, in criticising 'the high game that my Lady Castlemaine plays at court', told his patron Lord Sandwich that it was something 'the people do take great notice of'. The diarist was therefore surprised, on seeing a crowd around her coach at a puppet show at Bartholomew Fair, that she was not abused. 'But they, silly people! did not know her work.' It is possible they did not recognise her, for certainly her reputation was well enough known, as was demonstrated the following year during the riot of London apprentices. Having pulled down some notorious brothels the apprentices made clear their view that the biggest brothel of all, Whitehall Palace, remained. The riot was followed shortly afterwards by the publication of a mock *Petition of the Poor Whores to the Most Splendid, Illustrious, Serene and Eminent Lady of Pleasure, the Countess of Castlemaine* asking for her support for 'a trade wherein your Ladyship has great experience'. All Barbara's fury could not prevent someone from publishing a mock *Gracious Answer*. It was not difficult to drag a court such as this into the gutter.

In spite of her reputation Lady Castlemaine remained incorrigible over her spending and proud of her influence over her royal lover, which she exerted by increasingly strident means. It was noticed that she became more and more 'disagreeable from the unpolished state of her manners, her ill-timed pride, her uneven temper, and extravagant humours'. There were often violent arguments but the love-struck Charles could not help coming back to her. Not that her tantrums prevented him from falling for other women. He developed a strong passion for his distant cousin, the exquisitely lovely Frances Stuart, sent over from France by his sister to be a Maid of Honour. Lady Castlemaine took up this fifteen-year-old charmer, but lived to regret it. Frances was of the type which has since become known as the dumb blonde. It was said of her that it was almost impossible 'for a woman to have less wit or more beauty'. Nevertheless, she had wit enough to preserve herself from the King who pursued her relentlessly. The fact that his pursuit availed him nothing served only to intensify his desires. Her technique, as Anthony Hamilton observed, was to 'inflame the King's passions, without exposing her virtue by granting the last favours'. Ambitious politicians such as the Duke of Buckingham, seeking to please the King, cultivated her and tried to make her change her mind, but without success. Eventually, tiring of the chase, she eloped with a young duke as a final means of escape. Since her marriage took place without the King's consent and against his wishes Charles banished her from the court. In time, as so often happened with his easy-going nature, his anger evaporated and she was allowed back as a Lady of the Bedchamber. *La Belle Stuart* was to achieve her place in history not as one of Charles II's many mistresses, but as the model for the figure of Britannia on the coinage of the realm.

The King's roving eye was well matched by Lady Castlemaine's. Her thirst for money was exceeded only by her sexual appetites. Not content with having conquered a king and holding him in thrall for years, she allowed herself to fall for other men, even to the extent of supporting some of them financially. She was later to confess naïvely to Charles: 'You know as to love one is not mistress of oneself', and to prove her point she had one affair after the other with whoever caught her fancy. Fastidiousness was not her greatest virtue. Peers of the realm and her own footmen were equally serviceable. William Wycherley, the young dramatist, was one conquest, much to the annoyance of the Duke of Buckingham whom he replaced. When she began a relationship with Henry Jermyn, the future Lord Dover, the King, says Hamilton, 'advised her rather to bestow her favours upon Jacob Hall, the rope dancer, who was able to return them than lavish her money upon Jermyn to no purpose'. She needed no encouragement, and Jacob Hall, said to be a combination of Hercules and Adonis, found new outlets for his athleticism in Lady Castlemaine's bed. She also seduced the penniless John Churchill, at this time described as 'a youth of most beautiful form and graceful aspect'. Churchill had little more than his appearance with which to launch himself on the world, but with that shrewdness which was in time to transform him into the Duke of Marlborough, he invested the money Barbara gave him and bought himself an annuity.

Charles II is supposed to have come across Churchill and Lady Castlemaine together in a compromising position from which the young lover dived for cover. 'I forgive you,' was the cuckold's reaction, 'for you do it for your bread.' But such a situation could not continue indefinitely. Some had suspected the paternity of certain of Barbara's earlier children, though Charles recognised them as his own. He refused however to accept her 1667 offering; her weakness for Henry Jermyn was a more likely explanation. And her last child, born in 1672, was reckoned to be Churchill's. However footloose Charles might be himself, and however easy going, he required certain standards of faithfulness. These standards Barbara increasingly failed to meet, and she had not even the tact to ignore Charles's own casual affairs with other women.

One of those who attracted him was Winifred Wells, a Maid of Honour; as Hamilton put it, 'her father having faithfully served Charles the First, she thought it her duty not to revolt against Charles the Second'. (She was even rumoured to have 'dropped' a child at court while dancing.) But though she is described as having had 'the carriage of a goddess' it went with 'the physiognomy of a dreamy sheep', and the combination failed to sustain the royal passion for long. It was at this point that the King turned to the theatre where the interest he developed in low-born actresses gave Lady Castlemaine considerable scope for her talent for scorn. Charles himself had played an important part in restoring the legality of the theatre, and in setting up the two London playhouses in which women appeared for the first time on the English stage. According to Burnet it was the Duke of Buckingham who, to spite Lady Castlemaine, brought the King into contact with Moll Davis and Nell Gwyn.

Moll Davis, whose dancing Pepys had admired, first captured Charles's attention when she sang 'My Lodging It is on the Cold Ground'. As the wits of the time had it, she was not on the cold ground long before she was raised to a king's bed. The transformation, Pepys lamented, turned her into 'the most impertinent slut in the world'. It also brought her a house in Suffolk Street, a ring rumoured to be worth £600, and a daughter. This child was known as Lady Mary Tudor, and when she was fourteen she was married to the Earl of Derwentwater. So it was that Charles's daughter became mother of the tragic Earl who rose for the Stuarts in the 1715 Rebellion and was executed on Tower Hill.

Moll Davis did not remain in royal favour for long. A more lasting favourite was Nell Gwyn, 'pretty, witty Nell', who has gone down in folk history as a rags-to-riches heroine. In many ways she was the most deserving and least spoilt of the King's mistresses. Born about the time Charles was fathering his eldest son, she was raised in the slums of Drury Lane by a mother with a weakness for men and an even greater addiction to the bottle. As Nell later confessed, 'I was brought up in a bawdy house to fill strong waters to the guests'. In her early teens she was one of the girls engaged to sell oranges at the King's Theatre. Here her healthy good looks attracted the attention of Charles Hart, the great-nephew of Shakespeare, who carried on the family's theatrical tradition as an actor. Their relationship helped to launch her career as an actress. With her natural wit, and a complete lack of self-consciousness, she excelled in comic parts and Dryden, among others, was pleased to write plays specially for her talents. It was fashionable at this time for the young beaux to take actresses as their mistresses, and so Nell passed from Charles Hart, whom she called her 'Charles the First', to Charles Sackville, Lord Buckhurst, whom she dubbed 'Charles the Second' though when the King made himself 'Charles the Third' she was to insist that hitherto 'I was but one man's whore'.

Charles had seen her in a number of roles before he took her into the bed he had recently shared with Moll Davis. According to one story Moll had had the temerity to boast about her conquest, upon which Nell proceeded to feed her with doctored sweetmeats. That night, as a result, Moll found herself, during her assignation with the King, prostrate with diarrhoea. Moll Davis had pretensions to being a lady, which she obviously was not, and so she faded out. Nell on the other hand never pretended to be anything other than her own audacious natural self, and this was her continuing charm. Though she maintained her acting career for a time, proof of her new intimacy was provided by her withdrawal from the stage because of pregnancy, towards the end of 1669. The child was a boy, later the Duke of St. Albans. Her other son, born two years later, died as a child.

Though ordinary people did not generally begrudge the good luck of Mistress Nellie, as she was usually known, many in the higher ranks of society were apt to look down their noses at her and to regard her reputation and uncouth manner as bringing no credit to the monarchy. Evelyn referred to her contemptuously as 'the comedian and apple-woman's daughter'. Certainly by now Charles II, in respectable people's estimation, had well earned the Earl of Rochester's description of him:

> Restless he rolls about from Whore to Whore,
> A Merry Monarch, scandalous and poor.

Walking with his Sovereign in St. James's Park near the house Nell had been given in Pall Mall, Evelyn was shocked to hear 'a very familiar discourse', between king and mistress, literally over the garden wall. In similar circumstances, near her house at Newmarket, poor Alderman Wright had his ears bombarded by a shocking discourse with Nellie calling 'Charles, I hope I shall have your company at night shall I not?'.

The King's new interest gave rise to hostile comment in the House of Commons when a tax on theatres was being discussed. When pro-Court members said this would be a tax on the King's pleasure, Sir John Coventry suggested that this pleasure lay more with the actresses than the plays. Afterwards Coventry was waylaid by ruffians and had his nose split open for his trouble. There was continuing criticism of the expense the liaison involved. Gilbert Burnet, who thought Nell 'the indiscreetest and wildest creature that ever was in a court', was one of those who believed she was 'maintained at vast expense' – 'The Duke of Buckingham told me, that when she was first brought to the King she asked only 500L a year, and the King refused it. But when he told me this, about four years after, he said she had got of the King above sixty-thousand pounds.'

Cibber's *Apology* valiantly defended her against such strictures. 'She had less to be laid to her charge,' it argued, 'than
any other of those ladies who were in the same state of
preferment: she never meddled in matters of serious moment,
or was the tool of working politicians; never broke into those
amorous infidelities which others are accused of; but was as
visibly distinguished by her particular personal inclination to
the king as her rivals were by their titles and grandeur.'

It is true that Charles gave her a pension of £4000 a year out
of rents from land in Ireland (not always promptly paid), and
that later another £5000 a year was added out of the Secret
Service fund. In addition she was given the freehold of a house
near Windsor Castle and leases of land in Sherwood Forest
(according to tradition – unsubstantiated – as much as she
could ride round before breakfast). At least in her case it could
be argued that she had given up gainful occupation in the
theatre for the King and ought to be compensated. For the
rest of her life she led a comfortable existence, but there is no
evidence that she was grasping like her main competitors. By
comparison with them, her income was small and, as she was
kind-hearted, her money often found its way into other
people's pockets. As a result she was generally in debt, the
more so after developing a taste for gambling at cards.
Occasional bounty from the King tided her over these crises,
but it was the knowledge that she lived continually on the edge
of a financial precipice that induced Charles to utter his
famous deathbed plea on her behalf.

If Nell Gwyn had played an influential role in politics she
might have fared better financially. Being good-natured she
would often put in a kind word for someone in trouble. The
Duke of Buckingham had thought it wise to cultivate her, and
she rewarded him not only with her friendship but by
defending him when he had aroused the King's wrath.
Similarly the Duke of Monmouth could rely on her to speak
up for him when he was in disgrace. Even so, her power to
influence events was limited. She was more effective when it
came to deflating the pomposity of current favourites. 'She
acted all persons in such a lively manner,' says Burnet, 'and
was such a constant diversion to the King, that even a new
mistress could not drive her away.' She was even known to
mimic Charles himself: 'Odds fish, what company am I got

27

into?' When, after having raised other mistresses to the rank of duchess, he one day congratulated Nell on her dress with the words 'You are fine enough to be a queen', her reply was 'And I am whore enough to be a duchess'. She never did receive a title herself and, according to tradition, it was only by using clever tactics that she obtained one for her son. 'Come here you little bastard,' she is said to have called to him in his father's presence. The boy became Duke of St. Albans only a short time before the King died. Like his mother he was poorly provided for by comparison with the others, and the Dukes of St. Albans have always remained comparatively poor relations among Britain's dukes.

The years which witnessed Nell Gwyn's rise to fame coincided with those of Lady Castlemaine's decline. Her arguments with the King became unbearable. 'He had,' according to her, 'never ceased quarrelling thus unjustly with her ever since he had betrayed his own mean low inclinations; that to gratify such a depraved taste as his, he wanted only such silly things as Stewart, Wells and that pitiful strolling actress whom he had lately introduced into their society.' She accompanied her outbursts with floods of tears and Medea-like threats to their children. Nevertheless Charles did not drop her either suddenly or harshly. First there was her move from the Palace when he set her up in Berkshire House, and then her elevation to Duchess of Cleveland 'in consideration,' as the official declaration stated, tongue in cheek, 'of her noble descent, her father's death in the service of the crown, and by reason of her own personal virtues'. He then increased her pension, and they agreed to go their different ways on reasonably amicable terms. Accepting her nymphomaniac tendencies Charles gave her the best advice he could: 'Madam, all I ask of you for your own sake is to live so in future as to make the least noise you can, and I care not who you love.' It was just as well that he did not care, for a succession of lovers, usually young ones, followed not only during the rest of the King's life but for many years afterwards, culminating in her remarriage in her sixties to a young man who not only maltreated her but who turned out to be a bigamist as well.

For some years after her break with the King she lived in Paris. Her influence turned out to be not quite at an end. She had an affair there with the English Ambassador, Ralph

Montagu, who insulted her when he transferred his affections to her daughter. To spite him Barbara revealed to Charles certain ambassadorial double dealings with the French. The King had him recalled and Montagu, spiteful in his turn, then revealed to the House of Commons the fact that Charles's minister, Danby, had been seeking French financial aid. Danby's impeachment and imprisonment followed. No one could claim that Barbara Palmer had been a force for peace and quiet.

In the remaining years of Charles's life, however, she and the King remained outwardly on friendly terms. They shared a common interest in their children whose interests the mother continued to pursue. She herself was never out of financial difficulties and Charles had to help her out from time to time. She was not excluded altogether from his court, though she no longer had pretensions to being *maîtresse en titre*. Her place had been filled by another.

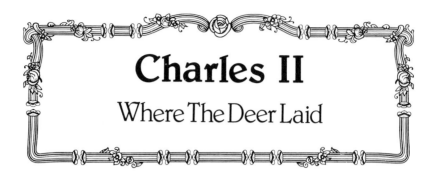

Charles II

Where The Deer Laid

The new star on the horizon was a French lady, Louise de Keroualle, whose ascendancy was to coincide with the more troublesome part of Charles's reign, when King and Parliament were at loggerheads for long periods amid a crescendo of anti-Catholic feeling. It was Charles's sister Henriette who first brought them together. Henriette, or Minette as she was generally known, had lived in France since childhood and had been married to Monsieur, the brother of Louis XIV. Neglected by her husband, who preferred male friends, she nevertheless became a force to be reckoned with. Her brother doted on her, and, for all the supposed influence of Charles's mistresses, the French Ambassador reported: 'The King often says that the only woman who has a real hold on him is his sister.' Realising the importance of this, in 1670 Louis XIV sent her to England to assist the French cause in clinching what became known as the Treaty of Dover. One of the secret terms of the treaty granted French subsidies to the English King, with the effect of making him less dependent on Parliament, in return for his announcing his conversion to Roman Catholicism when he judged it right. Whether Minette actually influenced Charles in these matters is doubtful; he was already pro-French and pro-Catholic. In any case, by retaining the right to announce his conversion when it suited him (which it never did) he got the best of both worlds.

The meeting of brother and sister at Dover had other important repercussions, for it was here that he met Mademoiselle de Keroualle who was one of Henriette's Maids of Honour. Louise had just turned twenty. He was forty and tiring fast of the overbearing Lady Castlemaine. The tradition is that at the end of her visit his sister sent Louise to him with her jewel box, asking him to choose some gem to commemorate their meeting, and that Charles's gallant reply was that the only jewel he coveted was the Maid of Honour.

When Minette died only a few months later Charles was heartbroken, and invited Louise de Keroualle to come over to England as one of the Maids of Honour to Queen Catherine. Louis XIV, himself open to persuasion by his own mistresses, perhaps believed that, with Charles's well-known weakness for women, this provided him with an excellent opportunity to exert influence at the English Court. He therefore pressed Louise to go. That the young Maid of Honour might influence the King was a view shared by the Duke of Buckingham, who took it upon himself to initiate arrangements to bring her over. Unfortunately these arrangements were bungled and it was left to Lord Arlington to complete matters.

She was closely scrutinised when she arrived. Her looks, with her round moon face, struck many English eyes as somewhat insipid. Evelyn had been expecting much of 'that famed beauty' and instead found her 'childish, simple and baby-faced'. But others thought her 'wondrous handsome'. Certainly Charles was swept off his feet. Her manners were appealing, her Breton background was aristocratic, even if the family fortune had disappeared, and there was more that was ladylike and soothing in her demeanour than in any of the previous royal favourites. Not for her the termagant approach of Barbara Palmer – when Louise was crossed she was apt to feign illness or burst into tears. ('The weeping willow' was the deflating nickname given her by the observant Nell Gwyn.) Quiet and cultivated, as well as attractive, she came as a tonic to the nerves of a king now approaching middle age.

But for once he did not have an easy conquest. Either she played hard-to-get or, more likely, being a respectable girl with a religious upbringing and reasonable marriage prospects, she was reluctant to embark on a career that was both unpalatable and uncertain. For a year she held out against all pleas. The King's ministers were just as anxious as their master that he should succeed. Arlington for one, though himself respectable and decorous, was most concerned that the King should have his way, especially as he was convinced that the affair would be harmless. He confided as much to the French Ambassador:

> My Lord Arlington told me recently that he was very glad to see the King his master attached to her for although His Majesty is not disposed to communicate his affairs to women, nevertheless as they can on occasion injure those whom they hate and in that way ruin much business, it was better for all good servants of the King that his attraction is to her, whose humour is not mischievous, and who is a lady, rather than to comediennes and the like on whom no honest man could rely, by whose means the Duke of Buckingham was always trying to entice the King in order to draw him away from all his Court and monopolise him.

It was therefore a feather in Arlington's cap when it was at his house at Euston, where they were all staying for the Newmarket races, that the matter was resolved. Either as a joke, or to salve Louise's conscience, the couple went through a form of mock marriage. A shocked John Evelyn recorded: 'The fair lady was bedded one of these nights, and the stocking flung after the manner of a married bride.'

After that first night at Euston Louise de Keroualle, soon to become Duchess of Portsmouth, began a special relationship with Charles II which was to last the rest of his life. To him she became 'my dear life' – 'I love you better than all the world besides'. This did not mean that he was faithful to her, annoying though she found this to be. He was naturally so polygamous that fidelity was a strain he was not prepared to impose upon himself. But through thick and thin, and in spite of numerous rumours to the contrary, she remained the first in his affection.

On her part, as Burnet had to admit, 'she studied to please him and observe him in everything'. In this she was assisted by her intelligence and good taste. Her fashionable apartments in Whitehall Palace became a quiet meeting place where he could relax. These rooms, torn apart and rebuilt several times, cost the country a small fortune and as early as 1675 Evelyn noted that they were ten times more luxuriously furnished than the Queen's. On another visit eight years later he was struck, not so much by the sight of the mistress in her dressing-gown having her hair combed in the presence of the King and his hangers-on, as by the abundant evidence of 'the riches and splendour of this world, purchased with vice and dishonour' – 'the new fabric of French tapestry, for design, tenderness of work, and incomparable imitation of the best paintings, beyond anything I had ever beheld...Japon cabinets, screens, pendule clocks, huge vases of wrought plate, tables, stands, chimney furniture, sconces, branches, braziers &c....all of massive silver, and without number, besides of his Majesty's best paintings'.

Unfortunately, the cost of the new Duchess of Portsmouth was to prove no less than the cost of Lady Castlemaine, now Duchess of Cleveland, with whom she shared a taste for gambling as well as for worldly possessions. It is true that some of the money came from gifts or bribes from those, including ambassadors, who sought her influence with the King. Ministers, too, found it a useful safeguard to grease her palm; though they might feel her power as a positive influence was limited, nevertheless she might prejudice the King against them. Danby, for instance, passed £55,000 to her over a two-year period, with the result that she did not scruple to support him, even against the French Ambassador. But the largest amounts of money came from the King, either directly or from funds at his disposal. At an early stage she was given a pension of £10,000, to be paid out of the revenues of land in Ireland. A few years later he granted her an annuity of £8,600 to come out of the excise duties. Then there was £1,000 a year out of the revenues of the First Fruits (paid for by the clergy!), a shilling on each cauldron of coal shipped from Newcastle, and *ad hoc* sums paid to her out of the Secret Service fund. Money was to be made from the sale of royal pardons. And there were frequent gifts of jewels.

This liberal pandering to a mistress once again had its repercussions. 'The more politically minded,' reported the Venetian Ambassador, 'dwell on the quantity of gold which the King has given and which he lavishes daily upon his most favoured lady.' The House of Commons, inclined to be increasingly critical of the King when he asked for money, again had a shrewd idea of what was going on. In 1673, when more money was required for the Dutch War, one of the grievances discussed was the suggestion that £400,000 had been given away since the previous session, a great deal of it to the Duchesses of Cleveland and Portsmouth. This added to the growing difficulties Charles was having over his suspected pro-French and pro-Catholic leanings which in turn led to his proroguing Parliament and living for as long as he could on money from other sources.

Altogether it was to prove a grave disadvantage to him that this long-lasting mistress was herself a Papist and a French-woman. Even her name troubled the insular English. To the educated Evelyn she was at various times Quierovil, Quierwill and Quirreval, while to less educated Londoners Mrs Carwell sufficed. She was a gift to the King's opponents, and someone even managed to stick on her apartment door the message:

> Within this place a bed's appointed
> For a French bitch and God's anointed.

Such views percolated down to the mass of the population, as was discovered when Charles's last Parliament met at Oxford, still a Royalist stronghold. Here it had been assumed that the atmosphere would be peaceful, but the appearance on the streets of what was thought to be the Duchess of Portsmouth's coach almost caused a riot. Only when Nell Gwyn cheekily thrust her pretty head out of the window and cried 'Pray good people be civil, I am the *Protestant* whore' did a tense situation turn to laughter.

Nell had other ways of deflating her lofty rival. When, for instance, she tired of seeing Louise going into mourning for deceased French noblemen in order to emphasise her aristocratic connections, Nell herself appeared one day in mourning clothes. 'Have you not heard,' she replied when asked the reason, 'of my loss in the death of the Cham of Tartary?' It must have been galling for the proud Duchess that she never managed to wean her lover away from the plebeian and vulgar Nellie. Nell's attitude was 'If she be such a lady of quality, why does she demean herself to be a courtesan?' Says Madame de Sévigné in one of her letters: 'The actress is as haughty as Mademoiselle: she insults her, she makes grimaces at her, she attacks her, she frequently steals the King from her, and boasts whenever he gives her the preference.' She even questioned her rival's political influence. 'Why is it,' she asked the French Ambassador, 'that the King of France does not send presents to me, instead of the weeping willow? The King is a thousand times fonder of me than her.' The conversation, however, then changed from intrigue to something more in Nell's line, culminating in her showing how rich and clean were her underclothes and 'certain other things that were shown to us all'.

It was certainly Louis XIV's hope that the Duchess of Portsmouth would remain a permanent French influence at the British court. French ambassadors acted as if she were, and their despatches home provide some of the best accounts of what went on behind the scenes at Whitehall in these years. Backstairs intrigue was much in evidence. From the time of her arrival in England her apartments were the focus of attention of successive French envoys who regarded her as their natural ally. It was their practice to visit her daily, and often Charles found it convenient to have confidential discussions with them in her rooms. (Ministers, too, continued the practice of Lady Castlemaine's day, and used to congregate there, and when, for instance, there was a political crisis caused by the King's serious illness at the height of the campaign to exclude his brother from the succession, it was in Louise's apartments that the ministers met.) But on the whole French efforts were out of all proportion to their success. There is no proof that what was whispered to Charles on his pillow or begged of him in some tête-à-tête had any effect on his policies: he knew where he wanted to go and continued to steer in that direction regardless of bedroom intrigue. Besides, he knew what was afoot, of the flattery and bribery of which the French were masters, and thus forearmed was able to put any suggestions coming from that quarter in proper perspective. Accordingly, when the French Ambassador primed the Duchess to use her influence against the proposed marriage of William of Orange to Charles's niece Mary, the King turned a deaf ear and continued to agree with Danby as to its desirability.

In any case, though Louise was a natural intriguer, her eye was on the main chance. Her own interests came first, then those of Charles, with France coming third. It is true an

35

ambassador might inform Louis 'She has shown great, constant and intelligent zeal for your Majesty's interests, and given the numberless useful hints and pieces of information', and that a good deal of confidential information got back to the French court in this way, but she was equally adept at putting Charles's point of view to the French. And she was not always in the know; when, for instance, Charles and the Ambassador were discussing the need for fresh French subsidies she knew nothing of the negotiations. When it suited her she took her own line. Thus, when the question of selecting a second wife for the Duke of York arose, she supported the British idea of a non-French bride. Then Louis' envoy complained bitterly of her being 'on all occasions so ill-disposed for the service of the [French] King and showing such ill-humour against France'.

On such occasions her political judgement and instinct for survival outweighed other loyalties. She knew for instance that Louis' candidate in this case, being both French and a Catholic, aroused the two deepest prejudices in the English mind. Unfortunately for Louise, as she found to her cost, these prejudices tended to centre round her own person. To some extent this was unfair. As regards religion, the King's own Catholic beliefs had been formed long before he met her. Moreover, though she was a loyal Catholic, she was no fanatic. The son who was born nine months after the stocking had been flung at Euston, and whom Charles made Duke of Richmond, was brought up a Protestant. Similarly her lover's views on foreign affairs owed nothing to what she had to offer. Yet the fact that the King's foreign policy was suspect, his heir a known Catholic, and to crown all his principal mistress both Catholic and French, made Charles II's life in the second half of his reign much more difficult than it might otherwise have been.

For, not surprisingly, in these later years, when wild rumours of popish plots abounded, such matters came in for considerable attention. One outcome was that when Lord Shaftesbury was in the ascendant against the court, his supporters arranged that a Grand Jury should present bills of indictment, not only against the Duke of York as a Roman Catholic, but against the Duchess of Portsmouth as a 'common whore'. Only swift action by the King in discharging the jury prevented the mischief from proceeding. Nevertheless the prestige of the monarchy suffered as these moves became widely known.

It was in this kind of situation that the Duchess's instinct for self-preservation asserted itself. Events in the year 1680, in particular, were to prove that she was much more of a trimmer than her lover. With the increase in anti-Catholic feeling reaching such frightening proportions Louise put her own safety first and endeavoured to make her peace with the opposition. In the words of James II's autobiography she 'made her conditions with my Lord Shaftesbury and the factious party'. In doing so she was patently currying favour with those bent on excluding James from the throne. She also dismissed her Catholic servants, and even sent a message to the arch-Protestant William of Orange telling him she was 'more his friend than he imagined'. Her overtures to Shaftesbury and his principal colleagues paid dividends, for when Parliament met later that year they headed off the attempts of their less restrained supporters to denounce her and her supposed power.

In all this she must have fallen in the King's estimation. For Charles showed his true mettle in bending to the wind to the extent of sending his brother into exile, but in refusing to exclude him from the succession. He was equally adamant in refusing to countenance the suggestion that his eldest son, the Duke of Monmouth, who let himself be used as the rival Protestant Duke to the Catholic Duke of York, was legitimate. 'I'd rather see him hanged at Tyburn' was the reaction of the King to the suggestion that he announce that he had been married to Monmouth's mother; instead he denied in Council the 'false and malicious report'. These were years when Charles must have regretted bitterly his youthful liaison with Lucy Walter. Although he loved Monmouth his life was made almost impossible by his son's behaviour.

When Charles sent his son into exile Monmouth blamed the Duchess of Portsmouth for being in the vanguard of those ranged against him. But even Nell Gwyn, who had always been willing to speak up for him, was unable to persuade Charles to alter his view. Not that the Duchess's current view of the Duke of Monmouth cut much ice with the Duke of York. After her previous behaviour he decided that she was 'never to be trusted'. He could not forget that she had played him 'a dog's trick'. However, in the last years of the reign Louise was shrewd enough to recognise James as the rising sun and to seek to help his cause whenever she could.

Curiously her political shifts and lack of courage do not seem to have altered the King's affection for his mistress, despite various rumours to the contrary. Not that she was ever without competition. There was particular fluttering in the diplomatic and ministerial dovecotes with the arrival in London of Hortense Mancini, Duchesse de Mazarin, a niece of the great Cardinal Mazarin. During Charles's exile, marriage between the two of them had actually been mooted, but since then she had married disastrously elsewhere and separated from her husband. 'An extraordinary beauty and witt, but dissolute,' John Evelyn decided, 'all the world knows her storie.' Charles was entranced and could not see enough of her. The Duchess of Portsmouth became quite tearful about the affair and the effect it might have on her future. Her apprehensions were shared by the King's ministers, who were divided over which horse to back, and by that most sensitive of barometers the French Ambassador, who was for ever trying to gauge the relative influence of various mistresses and ministers around the King. Versailles, itself so much subject to the power of the distaff especially with the advent of Madame de Maintenon, advised its envoy to hedge his bets by paying court to the new arrival. Hortense, as it turned out, was no more capable of being faithful than Charles himself, and when a former acquaintance of hers, the young Prince of Monaco, arrived in London it became known that she had found a new lover. Though relations remained friendly, Charles's ardour quickly cooled, as it was apt to do in the face of competition. So Louise continued to reign supreme.

Later, when she was still in her early thirties but Charles was fifty-three and beginning to feel his age, it was her own wandering eye which caused trouble. It wandered in the direction of another French visitor to England, Philippe de Vendôme. Burnet goes as far as to say that Charles, 'coming himself a little abruptly on them saw more than he himself had a mind to see', and gave Vendôme his marching orders. Louise was wise enough to acquiesce. The episode appears to have convinced Charles that life without her would be impossible, 'to such a pitch,' as Burnet puts it, 'that after this the

King kissed her often before all the world, which he was never observed to do before this time'.

His physical needs were now less than they had been, but he was as dependent as ever on female company and consolation, his time being largely divided between the Duchess of Portsmouth and Nell Gwyn. Evelyn was present at one typical evening at court in the midst of 'the King's natural children, viz: the Lady Lichfield, Sussex, Duchess of Portsmouth, Nelly and co: concubines and catell of that sort, as splendid as jewels and excess of bravery could make them'. Early in 1685 he witnessed a similar scene. 'I am never to forget the inexpressible luxury and profaneness, gaming and all dissolution, and as it were total forgetfulness of God (it being Sunday evening)... the King sitting and toying with his concubines, Portsmouth Cleveland and Mazarine... a French boy singing love songs... Six days after all was dust.'

The King's collapse was sudden. One evening he had supper as usual in the Duchess of Portsmouth's apartments. Then with a male attendant 'slept in a room with a great grate filled with Scotch coal, a dozen dogs came to our bed and several pendulums that struck at the half hour and not all going alike it was a continual chiming'. Next morning he collapsed, though it took several days and the assistance of his doctors for him to die, the 'unconscionable time a'dying' for which he apologised. During part of that time his bastard sons, excepting the exiled Duke of Monmouth, were present, but for decency's sake he saw nothing of his mistresses. His neglected but still devoted Queen busied herself around his deathbed. 'He entreated the Queen to pardon him,' says Evelyn who added tartly 'not without cause'. He begged his heir, the Duke of York, 'over and over again' to look after the Duchess of Portsmouth 'and that Nellie might not starve'. ('I do not hear,' reflected Evelyn sadly, 'that he said anything of the Church or his people, now falling under the Government of a Prince suspected for his religion.') Of Louise Charles declared 'I have always loved her, and I die loving her'. According to the French Ambassador, she on her part performed one last act for him. She reminded the Duke of York that Charles was a convinced Catholic and must therefore wish to receive extreme unction from a Roman Catholic priest, something which James managed secretly to arrange.

After her lover's death the resilient Louise survived another fifty years. She was never to be without her financial difficulties. She had managed to spend a vast sum of money with little to show for it other than a French estate. At first a small pension from James helped her to cope and to live in France in some comfort. When that pension stopped after James's flight Louis XIV came to the rescue. Finally she came to depend on a grant from the Regent Orleans, given 'in consideration of the great services she has rendered to France'.

Poor Nellie did not actually starve when the King died, but her creditors descended upon her unmercifully, putting her at risk of being sent to a debtors' prison. An appeal to James was not in vain. To his credit, he settled her immediate debts and gave her a pension of £1500 a year. He was to come to the rescue again two years later. (Apparently all he asked in return was that her son should become a Catholic, but here he was out of luck.) With Charles's death, however, the light seemed to go out of her life: as she told the new King, 'he was my friend and allowed me to tell him all my griefs, and did like a friend advise me and told me who was my friend and who was not'. Though still only in her thirties, she survived Charles by only two years. She left behind her a legend, the only royal mistress in English history to provoke popular affection. To her credit she never looked at another man. 'She would not,' she told a hopeful suitor in the colourful language that was part of her charm, 'lay a dog where the deer laid'.

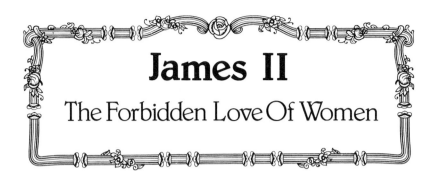

James II
The Forbidden Love Of Women

'I do not believe,' Charles II once told the French Ambassador, 'there are two men who love women more than you and I do, but my brother, devout as he is, loves them more.' If a disturbed youth was in any way to blame for this phenomenon then James's had, if anything, been even more disturbed than that of Charles. Born in 1633, he was only nine years old when his father's quarrel with Parliament obtruded on his life, and he was twenty-six by the time his brother was restored to the throne. To his uncertain existence during those formative years one must look for at least a partial explanation of James's peculiar life and character.

At first glance it might appear to have been an exciting adventure. As a boy he was, for instance, at his father's side at the battle of Edgehill. Having been taken prisoner by Parliament, he escaped abroad dressed as a girl when he was fourteen. But more often tragedy marred his life, with the loss of his home and family life while he was still a child, his father's execution a few years later, then life in exile with a domineering mother, so little money that at times he even went hungry and in ragged clothing, moving on when he was not wanted, and over all the apparent hopelessness of ever returning home.

Cast into such unsettled circumstances he did what many young men without roots have done, and joined the army to give his life stability and purpose. At the age of eighteen he gave his services to the great Turenne, fighting on the side of

41

Louis XIV. Later he was to fight for Spain. James made a good soldier, dedicated, hardworking and brave, if somewhat stiff and humourless. His soldiering was to colour his outlook on life. Whereas his brother became the arch-diplomatist, adept at side-stepping difficult issues, James learned different lessons. When he saw a difficulty he threw himself into it, as into battle. This was to be his eventual undoing.

As he developed into a tall young man, darkly good-looking though with a melancholy expression, he kept clear of more than casual relations with women. In the retrospect of a pious old age he was to lament his past life: 'Nothing has been more fatal to men, and to great men, than the letting themselves go to the forbidden love of women,' he was to advise his son; 'of all the vices it is the most bewitching, and harder to be mastered if it be not crushed in the very bud.' But in his hot youth there is no evidence of any overwhelming desire to crush it in the bud. Nothing could have been more natural for a young man with a shattered family background, on poor terms with his mother, and now an itinerant soldier, than to throw himself into the arms of bewitching creatures. There was one half-hearted effort on his behalf to negotiate a marriage to the heiress of the Duc de Longueville, but as a penniless Englishman with apparently no prospects he would have been a poor catch. There is no evidence of any permanent female entanglement till he met Anne Hyde, only daughter of Edward Hyde, future Earl of Clarendon, the lawyer turned politician who was Charles II's mainstay in exile.

Edward Hyde had seen enough of the manners and morals of courts to make him wish to keep his daughter well away from them. It had therefore been contrary to his wishes that she was appointed Maid of Honour to the Princess of Orange, the sister of Charles and James who became mother of the future William III. It was as Maid of Honour that Anne first met James. She was nineteen, and though never a beauty she had enough of the bloom of youth to make her attractive, especially as she lacked competition in the Dutch court. What is more, she had a liveliness and gaiety which James himself lacked but which he found attractive in women. As his autobiography was to explain, she had 'wit and other qualities capable of surprising a heart less inclinable to sex than was that of his Royal Highness in the first warmth of his youth'.

Among those other qualities was the ability to say no. Her rejection of his advances did credit to a girl brought up by careful parents and conscious of her vulnerable social position. Her aloofness merely inflamed his desire, and he found that the only way to achieve his ends was to go through a form of marriage with her. This took place in secret in the autumn of 1659 at a time when his future, as the impoverished younger brother of an exiled Pretender, made his action understandable and, indeed, of no very great importance. Six months later came a revolution in his fortune, and James was riding at his brother's side on the triumphant return home.

Soon Anne too returned, and informed James that he was shortly to be the father of her child. In the light of his new position as heir to the throne, his marriage to Anne Hyde seemed a complete *mésalliance*. In an attempt to get him out of his predicament some of his friends, led by Charles Berkeley, came forward with preposterous suggestions that Anne had played fast and loose with them, and to his discredit James appears to have been willing to have accepted these stories in order to slide out of his responsibilities. His own mother was against the match. Anne's father, now Lord Chancellor, was later to be accused of promoting this fertile marriage of his daughter and then of arranging that the King marry an infertile princess. In fact he fervently denounced his daughter as a common strumpet and threatened to turn her out into the street. Only Charles appears to have kept his head. Having examined the history of the case he decided his brother 'must drink as he has brewed' and arranged for the match to be formalised. This ceremony took place in September 1660. The child arrived seven weeks later, the first of eight babies to be born in under eleven years. Only two girls, Mary and Anne, survived, each to become Queen.

As Duchess of York, Anne Hyde fulfilled her role better than anyone had dared hope. 'It is,' a foreign observer remarked, 'as if she were of the blood of kings.' Indeed it soon became obvious that she was of a domineering disposition. Pepys, whose work at the Admiralty when James was Lord High Admiral meant that he took a close interest in the York household, tersely observed that the husband 'in all things but his cod-piece is led by the nose by his wife'. The exception was an important one. Gilbert Burnet, who noted that the Duke was 'perpetually in one amour or another without being very nice in his choice', once asked him whether he had seduced the nun responsible for his conversion to Roman Catholicism. She was 'no tempting object' was James's reply. But all the evidence points to his being easily tempted. 'He was the most unguarded ogler of his time,' declared Anthony Hamilton, whose own sister was singled out for this treatment. James 'ogled her with great assiduity'. He would, after a day in the hunting field, corner her at court. 'There it was that, not daring to tell her what lay heavy on his heart, he entertained her with what he had in his head, telling her miracles of the cunning of foxes and the mettle of horses, giving her accounts of broken arms and legs' – till he dropped off to sleep.

Elsewhere his ogling soon led to other things. Says Hamilton, 'The Duke of York, having quieted his conscience by the declaration of his marriage, thought that he was entitled, by his generous effort, to give way a little to his inconstancy: he therefore immediately seized upon whatever he could first lay his hands upon, this was Lady Carnegy, who had been in several hands.' Lady Carnegie appears in Pepys' Diary as a lady who was 'most devilishly painted' and whose husband after a time 'did get out of her that she did dishonour him and so bid her continue', Lord Carnegie's revenge being that she gave the Duke of York 'a clap'. (Lord Carnegie later denied the whole thing.)

Soon it was Lady Chesterfield who, to her husband's intense annoyance, became the object of ducal attentions. James's hand was observed to wander over her person whilst the Queen played at cards. On seeing Lord Chesterfield spying on them the Duke, says Hamilton, 'almost undressed my lady in pulling away his hand'. Afterwards the Chesterfields made a hurried withdrawal into the country. Pepys, also having heard how the Duke was 'smitten in love with my lady Chesterfield', was therefore surprised to see the Duke and Duchess of York at the theatre soon after this 'kissing and leaning upon one another'. Lady Falmouth attracted the Duke's attentions for a while but she proved hard to pin down. Mary Kirke, another Maid of Honour, appears to have been more accommodating but with her James to his chagrin found himself competing with his nephew the Duke of Monmouth. Later Goditha Price, a 'small and stumpy' Maid of Honour to the Queen, sufficed.

Pretty Lady Denham, whose husband was old enough to be her father, was willing to co-operate but on certain conditions. First she asked for a position in the Duchess of York's household. (The long-suffering Duchess was almost as reluctant as Queen Catherine had been with Lady Castlemaine.) Then Lady Denham, Pepys records, was fastidious in another way, 'declaring she will not be his mistress as Mrs Price, to go up and down the Privy-stairs, but will be owned publicly and so she is', James taking all his attendants with him when he visited her each day. Both Pepys and Evelyn objected to the spectacle of 'this bitch of Denham' being followed by the Duke 'like a dog' on public occasions.

Pepys was doubly annoyed that his master 'is gone over to all his pleasures again, and leaves off care of business, what with his woman, my Lady Denham, and his hunting three times a week'. To be fair to the Duke, his devotion to business, and especially as Lord High Admiral, was normally intense and far exceeded in application and consistency anything shown by his pleasure-loving brother. Nevertheless his inconstancy and hastiness in love certainly diminished his stature as heir to the throne. It was with a sense of relief, therefore, that after a few months Pepys heard 'the Duke of York does not haunt my Lady Denham so much; that she troubles him with matters of State, being of my Lord Bristoll's faction, and that he avoids'. (Bristol was a fierce opponent of James's father-in-law, Lord Clarendon.) Unfortunately Lady Denham, poor woman, was ill and died soon afterwards. According to one account the whole business sent her husband temporarily out of his mind, inducing him to go to the King saying he was the Holy Ghost.

James was said to be so moved by the turn of events that he declared he would never again have 'a public mistress', and Pepys even heard stories of women being procured secretly for him and spirited into his closet at Whitehall. Yet even before Lady Denham's death the Duke had entered into what proved to be a semi-permanent relationship, and once again the lady involved was a Maid of Honour, this time Arabella Churchill, aged seventeen. James liked them young. Anthony Hamilton, however, had such contempt for Arabella's looks as to find her new lover's passion barely comprehensible – 'a tall creature, pale-faced, and nothing but skin and bone . . . that ugly skeleton Churchill'. But she had a good figure, and what really fired the Duke's ardour was to see her clothes dishevelled after a fall from a runaway horse and to discover that 'limbs of such exquisite beauty could belong to Miss Churchill's face'. To some extent Hamilton was unfair. To judge from her portrait, Arabella Churchill appears attractive enough. Certainly she was able to retain her royal lover for a number of years during which she presented him with four children. Their eldest son, James FitzJames, became the famous Duke of Berwick, Marshal of France, who fought so valiantly for Louis XIV. By a curious twist of fate, the leading opponent of Louis by this time was Arabella's brother, John Churchill, Duke of Marlborough, and there can be little doubt that Arabella's influence with the Duke of York helped give her brother the start he needed in what was to prove a brilliant military career. That James helped Churchill get his commission did not stop the ambitious soldier from switching his allegiance to William III at a critical juncture in James's reign.

The fact that Arabella Churchill produced healthy sons is sufficient answer to the suggestions made at the time that the Duke of York was by now incapable of fathering healthy children. Throughout all his extra-marital affairs his wife, too, had had repeated pregnancies, but she failed to produce a male heir capable of surviving infancy. Altogether her married life became an unenviable one. For her solace, perhaps, she turned to Roman Catholicism like her husband, but she appears to have found greater comfort in excessive eating, becoming 'one of the highest feeders in England'. Her consequent plumpness contrasted strikingly with the leanness of her husband who, it was noticed, 'being excessively in the hurry of new fancies, exhausted himself by his inconstancy, and was gradually wasting away'. Nevertheless it was Anne who died prematurely, only six weeks after the birth of her last baby.

His unfortunate marriage to Anne Hyde and his continued partiality for extra-marital affairs did not discourage James from wanting to marry a second time. Indeed he was most anxious to do so, and a search soon started for a suitable bride, this time among the European princesses. Characteristically, he chose this moment to make a fool of himself once again, falling head over heels in love with Lady Belasyse, a seventeen-year-old widow of no great beauty with whom he went so far as to promise marriage. This time his brother Charles would have none of it. 'It was too much that he had played the fool once: that was not to be done a second time, and at such an age.' It was with some embarrassment that the lady had to be asked to agree that the offer be withdrawn.

The bride eventually selected was a princess of Modena, aged only fifteen at a time when James was forty. Moreover, Mary Beatrice was a Roman Catholic so devout that it had been her firm intention to take the veil, and it needed the Pope himself to persuade her that marriage to the Catholic heir to Britain's throne was a higher calling. They were married by proxy without having seen one another, an arrangement hurried on partly to forestall the anti-Catholic outcry anticipated when Parliament met. James's mistresses, who were generally Protestant, were tolerated without much fuss. It was his marriages that caused controversy. This one confirmed the fact of his own conversion to Catholicism, which was to cause infinite trouble in the rest of his brother's reign and his own.

When the child-bride arrived in England they were, as James put it, 'married and bedded that same night'. James could not have chosen his bride better himself, indeed he would probably have done less well. Mary Beatrice was to grow into a woman of striking beauty. In spite of his moral lapses she was also to show considerable loyalty to her husband, and, in time, great affection. He was delighted with her, even if his delight did not lead to complete fidelity. Soon a series of pregnancies such as had marred the life of his first wife recurred with this one, for many years with even less success. Like her predecessor, the new Duchess of York had to put up with James's continuous infidelities, and to learn to give the impression of placid acceptance of his peccadilloes. She knew from the beginning of her husband's attachment to Arabella Churchill, which continued uninterrupted. Indeed, the year after the marriage the mistress produced another healthy child.

After a year or two relations with Arabella cooled, and in 1677 she found herself a husband in Colonel Charles Godfrey with whom she was to enjoy a married life of nearly forty years. Soon tiring of being without a regular mistress, the next year James followed his old tradition and established a liaison with one of his wife's Maids of Honour. Catherine Sedley was the Protestant daughter of the rake, playwright and wealthy baronet Sir Charles Sedley. Like Mary Beatrice she was young enough to be James's daughter, but unlike the Duchess she had little in her appearance to recommend her. She was skinny and, it was said, 'squinted', probably from being shortsighted.

Her father had already tried using his money to make her the wife of John Churchill, but Churchill preferred the penniless beauty of Sarah Jennings. Why then did James fall for her? She may have been an easy conquest since, before she was sixteen, Pepys was describing her as 'none of the most virtuous, but a witt'. She herself could not account for her success: 'It cannot be my beauty for he must see I have none, and it cannot be my wit, for he has not enough to know I have any.' It must however have been her wit, or what the French Ambassador described as '*beaucoup d'esprit et de vivacité*', which attracted and retained James's attention. The relationship produced for him another family, though there is doubt as to whether the child known as Lady Katherine Darnley, whom James recognised as his daughter, was in fact fathered by him. Lady Katherine was to make a great match, becoming the formidable Duchess of Buckinghamshire, and took the greatest pride in her supposedly royal blood. Her mother, however, was known to have told her, 'You need not be so proud for you are not the King's but old Grahame's daughter', Colonel James Grahame having been Keeper of James's Privy Purse.

Charles II could not understand his brother's new-found devotion. Catherine Sedley, as her father's daughter, had a gift for repartee, and a certain hardness that went with it. The King enjoyed the repartee but it was obviously with Catherine's looks in mind that he uttered his famous remark that his brother was given his mistresses by his priests as a penance. Though James appears to have had a weakness for thin women and, according to Anthony Hamilton, was particularly fascinated by those wearing green stockings, his brother's barb was a little unfair. Charles was nearer the truth when he described his successor as 'stiff as a mule', and he was at least partly correct when he forecast 'He will lose his kingdom by his bigotry and his soul for a lot of trollops', or, according to another version, 'He will lose his kingdom through his religious zeal, and his soul through his unsightly wantons, because he has not even the niceness to like them beautiful'. Charles II apparently thought that the Almighty would condone illicit affairs providing the women were good-looking.

When the time came for James to succeed to the throne he took over peacefully enough except, ironically, for the trouble caused by the by-blow of Charles's own early years, the Duke of Monmouth. The young Duke invaded England and proclaimed himself King. The Battle of Sedgemoor ended his attempt and brought his life to a close under the executioner's axe. 'Thus ended this quondam Duke,' Evelyn recorded, 'darling of his father and the ladies ... of an easy nature, debauched by lust, seduc'd by crafty knaves.' Thus, following such an invasion, was James able to persuade Parliament to let him have the expanded army which was to overawe his subjects later in his reign. Thus Charles II's affair with Lucy Walter came to a bloody end.

The more businesslike approach which James brought to affairs of state at the beginning of his reign, and his declared intention to get rid of the vice and dissipation which had been regarded as the most shocking aspect of his brother's court, were widely welcomed. Whatever other doubts he may have had, John Evelyn, for one, was pleased with the 'more solemn and moral' court and the new King's lack of 'profaneness'. Even Louis XIV by this time was setting an example, having given up Madame de Montespan, and secretly married Madame de Maintenon. At first it appeared that James himself had turned over a new leaf. Catherine Sedley was moved from her Whitehall apartment and re-established in the house in St. James's Square formerly occupied by Arabella Churchill. James gave up seeing her, doubling her pension to £4,000 presumably as compensation. (By comparison with Charles II, James II's expenditure on his pleasures and weaknesses was to be sparse, with the result that more money was available for more dangerous uses.)

Before the year was out, however, the new King had succumbed to temptation, and he and Catherine Sedley were meeting again. Well might he confess to his son in later life 'with shame and confusion, I let myself go too much to the love of women which for too long gott the better of me: I have paid dearly for it'. Actually, as far as worldly power is concerned, James might have paid less dear had he taken more notice of this Protestant mistress and less of his wife and other Catholic advisers. Though some of Catherine's sharpest barbs were reserved for Roman Catholics there is no evidence that she influenced her lover. There were hopes that Anne Hyde's brother, the Earl of Rochester, as the most important Protestant minister, might find Catherine Sedley a useful ally, but this came to nothing.

It appeared at first that Catherine's influence was on the increase when, less than a year after his accession, James created her Countess of Dorchester. It seemed as if he might be drawing public attention to her as a preliminary to setting her up as the equivalent of the Duchess of Portsmouth. This caused immediate alarm in the Catholic camp. The news, says Evelyn, "'tis certaine the Queene took grievously ... so as for two dinners, standing neere her, she hardly eate one morsel, nor spake one word to the King'. Her co-religionists set to work on him, concentrating on his weakest flank – the effect his amour would have on the progress of Catholic conversions. James backed down. He now made a serious effort to terminate his relationship with his mistress. After standing her ground for some time Catherine at length agreed to withdraw to Ireland. She loathed the place and returned after only a few months. Once again it appears that the relationship with James was resumed, though probably in a less consuming fashion and with no political significance.

From now on, among women it was the Queen who had the greatest influence with her husband, and to clinch her claim to supremacy she surprised the world, after a long period of infertility, by producing a male heir when James was fifty-four. This was just at the time when the King's policies had begun to run into real difficulty, and by a curious twist of fate it was the arrival, at long last, of a healthy legitimate son which sealed James's fate. For it helped convince the opponents of the King's Catholic and autocratic policies that there was little hope of a peaceful restoration of Protestant influence in the next generation. Hence the eagerness with which the absurd rumour was put about that this was not the King's son but another child smuggled into the Queen's bed in a warming pan. Hence, too, the success of William III when he came over to assist the Protestant cause, and ended up by being installed joint monarch with James's daughter Mary.

James, with his wife and son, fled to France to spend the rest of his life as a pensioner of Louis XIV. During his attempt to regain his throne by an invasion of Ireland, the year after his departure, it was suggested by one writer that the habits of a lifetime had remained unchanged, and that he had two 'frightful scarecrows' in train. Be this as it may, the remaining years of his life appear to have been spent in unblemished domesticity and piety. He even came to reconcile himself to having lost his throne: it had purged him from a life of sin. If anything the opposite was true. Had he been set in a different mould, like that of his notoriously loose-living grandfather Henri IV of France, who had decided that Paris and a kingdom were worth a mass, James might have kept both his Protestant mistress and his kingdom by deciding that London was worth the Thirty-nine Articles.

His last mistress, now Countess of Dorchester, certainly showed no signs of guilt at continuing her life in England. Her father went so far as to boast his support for the new regime: 'Well, I am even with King James in point of civility, for as he made my daughter a Countess, so I have helped to make his daughter a Queen'. Catherine herself had no qualms about attending the new Queen's court, and, faced with Mary's coldness on seeing her father's ex-mistress, she had a typically brazen reply ready: 'Remember Ma'am, if I broke one Commandment *with* your father, you have broken another *against* him'.

She did not find it so easy to defend her material position. Her pension stopped and the grants of Irish land James had made her were called into question. Early in the new reign she established contact with James's exiled court, probably seeking relief from an acute shortage of money, though it is possible she was acting as a double agent for William III. At any rate William afterwards gave her a pension. 'Both the kings were civil to her,' she was afterwards wont to say, but 'both the queens used her badly.' Though the Irish Parliament was later to confirm the pension James had granted her, she was threatened by the English House of Commons with the loss of some of her land. This resulted in her going to the bar of the House herself to defend her case and, having a way with words, to win it.

In the intervening years she had scored another notable

51

victory in the outward form of respectability brought to her by marriage. When she was nearly forty she found a husband, a one-eyed Scottish baronet, Sir David Colyear, an officer in William's army. Sir David, as a contemporary cleverly put it, was 'very much a man of honour and nice in that way, yet married a Countess of Dorchester'. William III, however, continued to have a high regard for him and his military abilities and later created him Earl of Portnore. In spite of her advancing years Catherine produced for him two sons, one of whom was to be the ancestor of the famous Marquess Curzon of Kedleston. Perhaps the advice their mother gave these two boys when they went to school epitomises better than anything that coarse, earthy quality that was Catherine Sedley's strongest characteristic. 'If anybody call either of you the son of a whore,' she told them, 'you must bear it, for you are so, but if they call you bastards, fight till you die; for you are an honest man's sons.'

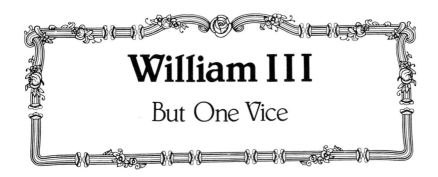

William III

But One Vice

Life for William of Orange was a troubled affair from the start. He was an only child and at his birth his father was already dead. His mother, a sister of Charles II, never felt at home in the Netherlands where her son soon found himself part of her struggle for power against his formidable grandmother. By the time William was ten his mother too was dead. The boy grew into manhood in an atmosphere of continuing intrigue and suspicion, learning to hide his real feelings. Nearly a century before, his great-grandfather, William the Silent, had successfully led the Protestant Dutch in their revolt against the Catholic tyranny of Spain. Afterwards the head of the House of Orange had continued to lead the country, not as King but as Stadtholder, an office which, as was borne out during William's minority, was not hereditary. It was only by playing his cards right that, under the threat of French invasion when he was twenty-one, William was made Stadtholder for life and Captain-General of the armed forces. In the face of overwhelming odds the asthmatic and never-robust young prince, old before his time, now showed that courage, tenacity and political statesmanship which were to characterise his whole life. Though he managed on this occasion to preserve his country, the primary occupation of his future years continued to be his determination to contain the expansionist policies of the French King.

William's early manhood, which other men with his wealth and social position might have spent in amorous dalliance, was therefore concentrated on intractable political and military problems. Instead of being locked in a mistress's arms he was locked in armed combat with his enemies. Indeed, the very sexuality of William III has been questioned. A clue to his real nature, normally fully under control, was given during a rare visit he paid to England when he was twenty. Characteristically his Uncle Charles proceeded one night to get him so drunk that young William gave way to his instincts. He tried to break into the apartments of the Maids of Honour who, it was said, were only 'timely rescued'. (At least Charles was never able to say of him, as he said later of Queen Anne's husband, 'I have tried him drunk and I have tried him sober and there is nothing in him'.)

It is true that after a childhood dominated by his mother and his grandmother William found the company of men congenial, and this has led to suggestions that he was homosexual. There is no evidence to prove such a charge. Both the particular friend of his youth, Willem Bentinck, and the friend of his middle-age, Joost Van Keppel, were strongly heterosexual. Much has been read into Gilbert Burnet's description of William: 'He had but one vice, in which he was very careful and secret.' But in his original version Burnet makes it clear that he was talking about mistresses, and comparing William's discreet behaviour with the notorious public womanising of his English uncles — 'If he has been guilty of any of the disorders that are too common to princes, yet he has not practised them as some to whom he is nearly related have done, but has endeavoured to cover them'.

As William advanced in his twenties the defence of his country remained his main preoccupation and he showed little inclination to marry, regarding this as something 'to be done at one time or other'. There was, however, a strong feeling among the Dutch that he should make a suitably impressive marriage to boost the prestige and strength both of his country and his family, and at the same time to perpetuate the Orange line. In England ministers and subjects shared a common desire to perpetuate the Protestant succession, at a time when it was clear that Charles II would never have legitimate heirs and that his brother and heir had been lost to the Catholic church. Charles himself was looking for ways to make amends for joining the French side in the Dutch War. His brother

James's elder daughter Mary, who with her sister Anne was being brought up a Protestant, was the obvious candidate for a marital alliance. William himself saw the political advantages of such a union, but before proceeding he took pains to enquire about Mary's character and conduct. He wanted not only a diplomatic marriage but an attractive and accommodating wife. No one knew better than he that, because of his own taciturnity, the difficulty he had in unbending in company, and his frequently itinerant life, domestic happiness would only be possible with a level-headed and tolerant spouse. Reports of Mary that he received encouraged him to proceed. Even so, when he eventually came to England and discussed the possibility of marriage, he showed both good sense and good feeling in refusing to commit himself till he had met his prospective bride.

Though Mary was only fifteen, William was pleased with what he saw. Still he refused to allow his matrimonial intentions to be used as a bargaining counter in discussions on England's difficult position in the Dutch War. First the marriage negotiations must be completed, and then other matters could be settled. Accordingly, under positive instructions from his brother, Mary's father, with considerable reluctance, gave his consent to the arrangement.

James's reluctance was as nothing to that of his tearful and homesick daughter, but she had no choice in the matter. She was at an age when she was full of romance and more interested in the intense 'Dear Husband' relationship with her adolescent female friend Frances Apsley. Now she was to be taken into exile by a thin bent cold man several inches shorter than herself, his frail looks comparing badly with her fine figure and early signs of what was to prove great beauty. So it was not the happiest of weddings which took place at St. James's Palace on William's twenty-seventh birthday, to be followed by a public bedding and Charles II's crude admonition 'Now nephew to your work! Hey! St. George for England!'

Once she arrived in Holland, Mary found she liked that clean and well-run land and the friendly Dutch people much better than she had expected. Soon, too, she was in love with her frail husband. William, of necessity, continued as an active soldier and was away from her a good deal. Even when at home he was inclined to be irritable and constantly preoccupied with affairs of state. This meant that Mary, who was naturally of a lively disposition, had to develop infinite tact and patience. No wonder she became a strange mixture of gaiety and melancholy combined with a strong dash of religion. She herself needed someone to lean on, and, though William was not a very ardent lover, nevertheless he was well-meaning and did not publicly keep a string of mistresses. Soon his wife was well satisfied with her lot. There was the additional consolation of pregnancy soon after their marriage. Unfortunately she was not as careful as she might have been, following William on one of his campaigns, and she had a miscarriage. Her father's advice to her to be 'more carefuller' of herself in future was unhappily not required as there were no further pregnancies. Still she continued to have hopes – and therefore William must have continued to give her cause to hope.

Perhaps the lack of children intensified Mary's desire to please her husband in other ways by trying to soothe away his cares. 'He comes to my chamber about supper time,' she told a confidante, 'upon this condition, that I should not tire him more with multiplicity of questions, but rather strive to recreate him, over-toil'd and almost spent, with pleasing jests, that might revive him with innocent mirth.' This approach helped cement a happy domestic relationship, an important factor in the political context of the time. For after her Catholic father Mary remained the Protestant heir of Great Britain. Following her was her sister Anne, then William himself. It is true that her father's second wife was young, and indeed had been heavily pregnant at the time of William and Mary's marriage, but Mary of Modena's pregnancies seemed doomed to miscarry. It was therefore important for the future of the throne, and the Protestant succession in England, that William and Mary should present a united front to the world. This, of course, was fully understood by William's enemies as well as himself, and it was in this knowledge that he nevertheless established a relationship with one of his wife's attendants.

The lady in question, Elizabeth Villiers, came from a family long connected with the English court. Her great-uncle, George Villiers, later Duke of Buckingham, had been James

I's favourite. Charles II's Lady Castlemaine was a cousin. Elizabeth's mother, Lady Frances Villiers, had been appointed by Charles as official governess to Princess Mary and her sister Anne. Elizabeth had therefore grown up in close proximity to the two princesses. Subsequently it was Mary herself who was responsible for bringing her future rival into contact with her husband, for Elizabeth and her younger sister were among those described as 'beggarly bitches all sueing for places' who were lucky enough to be included in the Princess's entourage when she went to Holland. Before long the younger sister made a great match by marrying William's friend Bentinck. Elizabeth remained single, though there was a Captain Wauchope who appears to have been making approaches to her. Then William himself entered the lists as her admirer and the Captain was heard of no more.

Unlike the Princess Mary who had developed into a woman of beauty, Elizabeth Villiers, as regards looks, had little beyond a good figure to recommend her. In later years at least her plain appearance was made worse by a perpetual squint. Her friend Dean Swift was to confess 'I always forget myself and talk of squinting people before her, and the good lady squints like a dragon'. But Swift admired her as 'the wisest woman I ever saw' and her intellect was almost certainly a key factor in attracting William to her. Whatever were Mary's other advantages, her mental powers were limited. Elizabeth Villiers, on the other hand, had an agile mind and a gift for conversation. She was a straight talker, which William liked, and a certain shrewdness shines through her dealings with him and others. She was interested in politics and was able to supply him with useful information picked up from her numerous contacts. Above all, she had a discretion approaching secretiveness and an ability to keep her own counsel which could not but appeal to a man like William.

It might be thought that the relationship was purely intellectual. 'One cannot imagine her arousing desire,' wrote one observer. It is however unlikely that the friendship always remained platonic, particularly as the lady's reputation was so completely compromised and she gave every appearance of being content that it should be. Certainly Mary took it very much to heart, even though she had earlier in life endeavoured to explain away her father's infidelities. ('In two or three years men are always weary of their wives and look to a Mrs as soon as they can get them.') Though William did not flaunt his new liaison, and excused his late nights by saying he was writing despatches, Mary soon knew what was afoot. As she later told him, for some years she 'kept her sorrow locked in her heart'. It was not, however, allowed to be locked away for ever.

In the months after James II came to the throne in Britain, some members of Mary's Household sympathetic to her father became active in conveying tittle-tattle to her in an endeavour to fan her jealousy. As a consequence of such gossip William, emerging late one night from the apartments of Elizabeth Villiers, found his wife waiting for him on the stairs. Her distress was far exceeded by his anger. He was convinced that people with ulterior motives were endeavouring to provoke a marital crisis. On recovering his composure he set about repairing the rift. 'What has given you so much pain is merely an amusement,' he told his wife, 'there is no crime in it.' Mary was more than willing to accept his protestations. William then went further. Suspecting a deeply laid plot he told her: 'If you believe the oath I now make to you before God, not to violate the faith I have given you, you will abandon your servants to my just resentment.' To Mary her relationship with her husband was paramount, and where he wanted to lead she was always willing to follow.

The interception of incriminating letters between James's envoy in the Netherlands, Sir Bevil Skelton, and Mary's Anglican Chaplain Dr Covell soon confirmed the existence of an intrigue against William and the sending back of intelligence to James. Covell was removed and James requested to recall Skelton. In Mary's Household her old nurse and two Maids of Honour were sent back to England for their part in the affair. The main effect of the whole business was not to tear husband and wife asunder. As Covell was to lament to Skelton, 'I fear the Prince will for ever rule the roast'. If anything it strengthened the resolve of husband and wife to stick together, but above all it worsened the already difficult relationship between the Catholic James and his son-in-law, the leading champion of Protestantism in Europe.

The most difficult aspect of the affair to resolve was what was to become of Elizabeth Villiers herself. All the evidence points to the fact that eventually Mary sent her back to

England with a sealed letter designed to ensure that she was not allowed to return. Elizabeth, however, suspicious of what was afoot, did not complete her journey and returned to Holland on her own initiative. Mary naturally refused to restore her to her old position in her Household, and Elizabeth's relations with her Bentinck relatives also became strained. William, it seems, continued to see her but their liaison was maintained with typical discretion.

Meanwhile, in England, James was fast alienating his own subjects. Britain's geographical position at Holland's back door, and his father-in-law's friendship with the newly aggressive French King, meant that William could not ignore what was happening in his wife's country. So when an invitation arrived from English nobles inviting him to lead an expedition to England it fell on fertile ground. Mary saw the matter from her husband's point of view. Whatever his treatment of her had been in the past, whatever his relationship with Elizabeth Villiers continued to be, William had cause to be grateful now for his wife's continuing loyalty and devotion to him. When, after his campaign had reached a successful conclusion, he insisted that there should be a joint monarchy of William III and Mary II, no one could have been more amenable than she. It was at his behest that on her arrival in her father's old palace she even forced herself to run cheerfully about, 'laughing and jolly, as to a wedding,' as Evelyn put it, 'as people do when they come into an inn,' in the words of Sarah Churchill.

Another arrival from Holland was Elizabeth Villiers, whose relationship with William was now re-established as discreetly as before. Not for her the official recognition afforded to mistresses in England in the previous reigns. She did not even get a place at court. Instead she took a house near William's home at Kensington Palace and made do with secret meetings, probably guessed at by the Queen. During William's absence in Ireland, at the time of the Battle of the Boyne, her attachment to him made her as anxious as Mary for his safety, so that when William's secretary came back early she pumped him for information. After William's victorious return malicious stories were spread about his liaison, how he spent many hours in Miss Villiers' company (there were even rumours that she was pregnant), showered her with riches and above all put the new regime in jeopardy by making the Queen desperately unhappy. Once again friends of James thought William's mistress the best means of breaking up his marriage and the joint monarchy that had enabled the Glorious Revolution to succeed.

In spite of rumours the amicable relationship between husband and wife continued. Indeed it was noted how, on returning from one campaign, the King forgot formality and kissed the Queen twice in public. With Mary a little attention went a long way. 'How kind the King is,' she enthused during another of his visits, 'how much more of his company I have had since he came home this time than I used to have.' She continued to hope for a child, and again William must have given her cause to hope. In contrast, it appears unlikely that at this stage his relations with Elizabeth Villiers were of a physical nature. The strait-laced John Evelyn had noted that, 'the impudence of both sex being now so great and universal, persons of all ranks keeping their courtesans so publicly, the King had lately directed a letter to the Bishops, to order their clergy to preach against that sin'. Had William himself been pursuing an illicit relationship it is hardly likely he would have taken such a step.

Elizabeth continued to be useful to him in other ways. Back on her home ground her value as a source of information and for sounding people out was enhanced. This was demonstrated after Mary had quarrelled with her sister Anne. (Curiously enough the first cause of dissension between them was the younger sister's wish to take over the Duchess of Portsmouth's old Whitehall apartments.) Elizabeth Villiers' contacts proved useful in enabling her to transmit to William details of what went on inside Anne's Household, which was completely dominated by the Churchills. (Eventually William heard that John Churchill was in touch with the exiled James, and he was dismissed from his command in consequence.)

Elizabeth was useful in other ways as well, as a fixer rather than as a positive political influence. When, for instance, the King was anxious to have the shrinking and neurotic but highly competent Earl of Shrewsbury as his Secretary of State, he used her to persuade the Earl to accept the proffered seals of office. As it happened, Miss Villiers was friendly both with Shrewsbury and Shrewsbury's mistress. But try as she might she failed in her mission. The fact that she told the Earl 'I know I am undone unless I succeed' shows how much she counted on her usefulness to William to help her maintain his friendship. Shrewsbury gallantly told her: 'When you, madam, have attempted to persuade, and have failed, you may conclude the thing is impossible.' Though Elizabeth may have helped to break the ice, Shrewsbury was actually more susceptible to Mary's charm, and when he was eventually persuaded to take office it was probably the wife rather than the mistress who had exercised the greater persuasion.

Mary showed sufficient lack of jealousy to sign the patents transferring to Miss Villiers 90,000 acres of James II's former Irish estates with a rent roll of £5,000 a year. Though William did not accord her official recognition, he was willing to show his generosity in this manner. Such grants did nothing to recommend him to his Parliament. But at least his female favourite was English. His male favourites, to whom he was happy to give titles as well as grants of money and land, were Dutch, and their presence and influence proved intensely irritating to his new subjects. Foremost among these favourites remained Bentinck, now Earl of Portland, whose dislike of the Villiers connection was only exceeded by his opposition to William's close relationship with Keppel, soon to be Earl of Albemarle. Keppel – who was a loose-living womaniser – was to William 'such a good boy', and it was his refusal to give him up which not only broke his friendship with Bentinck but also helped attract to him that reputation for homosexuality which did his name far more harm than Elizabeth Villiers ever did.

It was the unexpected death of Mary from smallpox when she was only thirty-two which finally brought the Villiers affair to an end. Mary died as meekly as she had lived, but it seems she left one last letter for her husband to read after her death. This letter was later destroyed but, according to someone who saw it, it consisted of 'an admonition to the King, for some irregularity in his conduct'. Mary had been a very religious woman and, though she affected indifference, the continuation of her husband's relationship with another woman had obviously continued to worry her. The Archbishop of Canterbury took it upon himself to speak to the royal widower – 'Sir, we must repent, and mend our life' – but this only brought on him a curt reply – 'Aye, Sir, we must mend our life, I must mend my life and you must mend yours'. Nevertheless, the Queen's death had bitten deeply into the conscience of the grief-stricken William and her letter had its effect. Having seen to it that Elizabeth Villiers was well taken care of financially, he took steps to break with her completely.

In the event she did not remain for long in the cold. A few months later she found herself a husband, an action which, if William did not promote, he certainly endorsed. Her new partner was George Hamilton, a younger son of the Duke of Hamilton, well-connected, well-to-do and good-looking. The King regarded him highly, created him Earl of Orkney and continued to promote his career in the army. (He was later to become Governor of Virginia, though apparently an absentee one.) The title was no doubt partly intended to enhance the position of the new Countess of Orkney, who thus started on a new career as she was approaching forty. It was not her style to feel guilty about the reputation she brought to her marriage. William's secretary says that she told her husband she had been 'on very good terms with a certain person, but that she did not wish to hear any reproaches or insinuations on that score'. And though some of his relations might look askance the new Lord Orkney made none. He settled down to a happy marriage and a fruitful one. In all the years of her liaison with William she had produced no offspring. Now, almost in her middle age, she was blessed with three children.

William, in the few years that remained to him, continued to lead a busy public and military life and an empty private one. Soon after the new eighteenth century dawned the 'little gentleman in black velvet', as the Jacobites called the mole which caused his horse to stumble, brought his fragile life to an end. Afterwards the lady whose reputation he had compromised lived on in state with her head high for another thirty years. One last glimpse of her in old age, witnessed by Lady Mary Wortley Montagu, was at the coronation of George II. It bears out all too well the fact that to the end Elizabeth Villiers never lost her self assurance. 'She that drew the greatest number of eyes was indisputably the Countess of Orkney,' recounted Lady Mary. 'She exposed behind a mixture of fat and wrinkles, and before a considerable pair of bubbies a good deal withered, a great belly that preceded her;

add to this the inimitable roll of her eyes and her grey hair which by good fortune stood directly upright, and tis impossible to imagine a more delightful spectacle.'

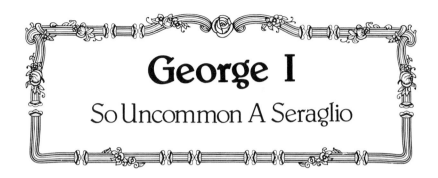

George I
So Uncommon A Seraglio

'Who would have thought that we three whores should have met here?' The question was addressed by James II's old mistress the Countess of Dorchester, alias Catherine Sedley, to Charles II's Duchess of Portsmouth, alias Louise de Keroualle, and William III's Countess of Orkney, Elizabeth Villiers – all meeting at the court of George I. Catherine Sedley's incisive mind appreciated the irony of the circumstances. Not only was George's dowdy, uninteresting apology for a court a most unlikely place for the three of them to meet, but that George himself should be the new King was something of a miracle. A distant relative of the later Stuarts, his only previous appearance in England had been in his youth, when he was considered a suitor for the hand of the Princess Anne. She had not appeared to suit him, and it was by her later marriage to Prince George of Denmark that Queen Anne owed the enormous family of children, all of whom predeceased her. The death of the last of them, shortly before William III died, had put the Protestant succession to the throne in jeopardy and led to Anne's distant cousin, the Elector of Hanover, becoming heir to the throne.

Anne's own reign of twelve years demonstrated the continuing importance of royal favourites in the life of the nation. Fat and middle-aged, bereft of a family other than her colourless and ineffectual husband, not inclined to take lovers, Anne turned for support to her female attendants. Foremost among these continued to be Sarah Churchill, Duchess of

Marlborough, whose influence with the Queen helped ensure that the Duke of Marlborough's largely Whig friends held high office. But in time Sarah's overbearing manner wore away the Queen's affection and another attendant, the future Lady Masham, replaced her in royal favour. At the same time, Tory politicians led by Harley and Bolingbroke were replacing the Whigs in government, and in the remaining years of the reign the Tories found the support of Lady Masham, assisted by various bribes, useful in maintaining their hold. They were inclined to overestimate the lady's hold over the Queen, for Anne was opinionated and stubborn. 'People think,' Lady Masham once confessed, 'I am able to persuade her to do anything I have a mind to have her do, but they will be convinced to the contrary one day or other.' They never were, and Lady Masham continued to do her best to bring pressure to bear up to the time of Anne's death in 1714.

When, with seeming reluctance, the new King George I left his Hanoverian dominions to take up his crown, he was fifty-four years of age. He arrived in England with a son and daughter-in-law but with no queen. The solution to this mystery lay in a strange story of love, intrigue and dynastic ambition. At the age of twenty-two George had married his sixteen-year-old cousin Sophia Dorothea. At first sight it might have appeared an ideal match, he in due course to inherit his father's electorate and she to come into her own rich inheritance. In fact from the outset the marriage had all the makings of disaster.

In George's family his bride was regarded not as an asset but as a danger that had to be neutralised. Her father, the reigning Duke of Celle, was the elder brother of George's father, and it was this elder brother who had originally been engaged to marry George's mother. As it happened, at that stage in his life the elder prince had been unwilling to settle down. Instead he had not only given up his intended bride to his brother but also, in order to improve the younger brother's prospects, promised never to marry. Afterwards he met a French noble-woman who became the love of his life. As she refused to live with him as a casual mistress, they entered into a formal arrangement to live as man and wife without benefit of clergy. Sophia Dorothea was the fruit of that agreement. Later there did take place a morganatic marriage between the parents and the child's legitimisation. Though there were formal safe-guards regarding the succession to the duchy of Celle by George's father, the whole affair was the cause of considerable apprehension and bitterness in the younger branch of the family. It was bad enough that inferior blood had been introduced into the line. Even worse was the fear in Hanover that, whatever the written safeguards, Celle would be lost to the family if Sophia Dorothea married elsewhere.

George's father was a realist and decided that a marriage between the cousins was the only way to secure the succession. As a dutiful son George did as he was bid. Arranged marriages were, after all usual among German princes. In this case, however, unlike many such unions which were cemented with the passage of time, the actual process of living together only made matters worse. For temperamentally they were feathers and lead. Sophia had inherited her French mother's vivacity. She was frivolous and somewhat vain, fond of clothes and jewellery. Above all she had a strong romantic streak. He was cold, cautious and calculating.

Though his taste was questionable, whatever female solace George required he obtained elsewhere. Since he was sixteen – when he had made his sister's governess pregnant – he had not been short of women friends. Nowhere were French habits more slavishly copied than in the small German courts. That the ruler and his male relations should have their mistresses, in the manner of Versailles, was a matter of course, and after his marriage George continued to follow the fashion in having a mistress and fathering illegitimate children. Where Sophia Dorothea made her mistake was in not accepting that such latitude was not allowed the wives of princes. As the Duchess of Orleans put it so succinctly: 'If wives were to lead the same sort of lives as their husbands, one could never tell with certainty who the true heir was in the family.' Accordingly, 'a wife's honour consists in having nothing to do with anybody except her husband, but there is no disgrace for men to have mistresses'.

Having produced two children by her neglectful husband, Sophia Dorothea ignored the convention and found a lover of her own. He was Count Phillip Konigsmarck, a Swedish soldier of fortune in the Hanoverian service, young, good-looking, rich, brave and flamboyant. As was proved by their highly indiscreet letters, some of which were intercepted, the affair developed into a grand passion culminating in a sexual relationship. At length the Hanoverian authorities decreed that such a state of affairs could not be allowed to continue and Konigsmarck was waylaid in the palace after one secret visit. He disappeared without trace. There can be no doubt that he was murdered. According to one story he was buried under the floor of the room where he was killed. More probably his body was weighed down with stones and thrown into the river.

Sophia Dorothea's wish to leave her husband for her lover had been made clear in her letters, and in the divorce case that followed this was construed as actual desertion. (Adultery would have brought the paternity of her children into dispute, and with it the rights of succession which were foremost in everyone's mind.) In the divorce decision, only George, as the innocent party, was given the right to remarry. His former wife was incarcerated in the Castle of Ahlden for the rest of her natural life, thirty-one long years. Where the dynasty was concerned George proved he could be hard and unforgiving. When he eventually arrived in England, though his former wife was still living, her name was never mentioned.

It was apparently with two mistresses in train that George I presented himself to his new kingdom. At first there seems to have been some reluctance among his intimate female friends to exchange the absolutism of the regime in Hanover for the uncertainties of Great Britain. The Countess Platen, the only one with any pretensions to beauty, was implacable in her decision to stay at home. (As she was a Roman Catholic perhaps this was for the best.) Hitherto the Platen family had been unsurpassed in the delicate services it had rendered to the Electoral House, co-operative to the point of nepotism and perhaps even of incest.

A former Countess Platen had been mistress to George's father. This earlier Countess, mother-in-law of the one who now remained behind, had had a daughter who had also established close links with the Electoral family. Having been married off to the Baron von Kielmannsegg, a Hanoverian diplomat, she was commonly thought to provide the same services for George as she did for her husband. Certainly she was the only one of his lady friends who appeared not to hesitate before coming to England.

Not that there was anything in La Kielmannsegg's appearance when she arrived to commend her as a promoter of royal passion. Having had some pretensions to beauty in her youth she was now, at the age of thirty-eight, a mountain of fat. So 'corpulent and ample' was she, explains Horace Walpole, that 'the mob of London were highly diverted at the importation of so uncommon a seraglio'. Taken as a boy to meet her, Horace was so overcome by what he saw that he carried a frightening memory of his experience with him for the rest of his life: 'Two fierce black eyes, large and rolling beneath two lofty arched eyebrows, two acres of cheek spread with crimson, an ocean of neck that overflowed and was not distinguished from the lower parts of her body . . .' A very uncommon seraglio indeed.

The other female influence in the King's life, a woman he had made his mistress back in Sophia Dorothea's time, bore the imposing name of Ehrengard Melusine von der Schulenburg. She, it was reported, had at first had reservations about coming to England at all. The English, she had heard, were in the habit of doing terrible things to their monarchs, and within a fortnight her lover might well be without his throne and even his head. However, as one who had long been an implacable enemy of the Platen family, she would have been the last to allow the Kielmannsegg woman to steal a march on her. Formerly a Maid of Honour to George's mother, Schulenburg was now aged forty-seven. Even in her youth she had had few pretensions to beauty to assist her cause. 'Do you see that scarecrow?' – George's exasperated mother had asked a visiting Englishwoman many years before – 'You would scarcely believe that she has captivated my son.' (Had George been asked to defend himself he could well have used the reply the dissolute Regent Orleans, with a hundred mistresses renowned for their ugliness, made to *his* mother: '*Bah! Maman, dans la nuit tous les chats sont gris*'.)

The fact was that Schulenburg was as tall and skinny as Kielmannsegg was round and ample. On their arrival in England they made a laughable combination – to be dubbed 'the Hop Pole and the Elephant' or 'the Maypole and the Elephant and Castle' – not in the least calculated to induce respect for the new King. 'Two considerable specimens of the King's bad taste and strong stomach,' declared Lord Chesterfield. 'The standard of His Majesty's taste as exemplified in his mistresses,' Chesterfield suggested, 'makes all ladies who aspire to his favour, and who are near the suitable age, strain and swell themselves, like the frogs in the fable, to rival the bulk and dignity of the ox. Some succeed, others burst.' The English were prejudiced against foreigners in any case, and the ungainliness of these two elevated camp followers turned dislike into disgust and ridicule. 'Good people, why you abuse us so? We have come only for your goods,' Schulenburg shouted in her imperfect English to the mob surrounding her coach. 'Yes, and for our chattels too,' came the inevitable reply.

To make matters worse George himself made little effort to ingratiate himself with his new people. The lack of a queen and a reliance on such unprepossessing substitutes did nothing to assist in the establishment of an attractive and prestigious court. The Prince of Wales and his wife did their best to do the honours and put a proper public face on the monarchy. But the King's own tastes were simple, and at fifty-four he refused to change the habits of a lifetime. Behaving more like the old soldier he was than the monarch of a great nation he dispensed with as much as possible of the old court ceremonial, hating even to receive ambassadors because of the formality it involved. The old rambling Palace of Whitehall, having been destroyed by fire in William's reign, George was quite happy to live modestly in St. James's or Kensington Palace, looked after by Mahemet and Mustapha his two trusted Turkish servants whose considerable influence soon became well known.

He preferred his pleasures, too, to be taken in private. He was happiest quietly associating with his German friends, male and female. He would visit Schulenburg in the afternoon or go with her to the opera (not in the royal box), or perhaps play cards with Kielmannsegg in informal surroundings where he could unbend. With such friends he could also converse easily, which must have been a great consolation to a man who failed to master the language of his new country. Still, such cosiness was a poor substitute in the public mind for what was lacking in this royal family.

In some respects the King's retiring, indeed secretive, nature did his reputation unnecessary harm. To those in the know it soon became clear that Schulenburg, greatly to Kielmannsegg's annoyance, had the greater influence. Though Kielmannsegg, belying her heavy appearance, could be vivacious and amusing, to the onlooker it appeared that the older lady's sobriety suited the old King better. For thirteen years, therefore, Schulenburg was seen to hold a position closer to *maîtresse en titre* than anyone since the Duchess of Portsmouth's time a generation before. Due to George's excessive reticence, however, what was not clear at the time was that probably *neither* lady was in fact his mistress.

Recent research has established beyond doubt that Kielmannsegg was his half-sister. No wonder she went to great lengths to deny that she had ever been unfaithful to her husband – incest is not a pleasant crime to be accused of. Poor lady, her efforts to defend herself only caused ridicule. For his part, George did little to dispel the mystery, presumably because he did not wish to sully the reputation of his House by proclaiming that his friend had her origins on the wrong side of the Electoral blanket. Unfortunately this forced most people to the conclusion that his interest in her must be sexual.

As for Schulenburg, it is likely that she was not the King's mistress but his wife. Even at the time it was whispered by those in the know that he had married her 'with his left hand', that is, morganatically. Horace Walpole and one of George's granddaughters, both of whom had good sources of information, believed this to be so. Of course morganatic marriages, whereby the non-royal wife does not assume her husband's rank, nor are her children in the line of succession, were quite common among European princes. In a similar situation Louis XIV had married Madame de Maintenon who had proved that a morganatic wife was capable of exercising more power than a fully-fledged one. In Britain up to this time such marriages were unknown. (When, two hundred years later, Edward VIII was to suggest he contract a morganatic marriage with Mrs Simpson he was told – wrongly it would now seem – that there was no precedent in this country.)

There can be little doubt, either, that there were daughters of George I's liaison with his Ehrengard. One girl, brought over from Hanover and passed off as Schulenburg's niece, was almost certainly her daughter by the King. When the child grew up she was created Countess of Walsingham and married the Earl of Chesterfield. Horace Walpole asserts that the later Viscountess Howe was Kielmannsegg's daughter by the King 'though she was not publicly owned'. She was almost certainly his niece. Whether niece or daughter, a title was as far as George would go – it never became the practice of the Georges to draw attention to their illegitimate relations.

From the hour of George I's accession, the most important question among those jockeying for position and power was the political role the new King would play. Whilst it appeared likely that he would co-operate closest with those Whigs who had engineered the Hanoverian succession, which groups among them would he favour? What policies would he seek to pursue? Who would have the greatest influence over him? What would be the best channel to get views across to him? At a period in constitutional development when, except in a crisis, the monarch's wishes as to who should be his ministers still counted for more than the views of the House of Commons, such questions were of great importance.

It soon became obvious that a man who was at once so suspicious, with such fixed ideas, well advanced in middle age and feeling so little at home in a strange country, would alter as little as possible the habits of a lifetime. This meant that the German ministers and diplomats who had helped him with his autocratic regime in Hanover continued to advise him in his new role. Led at the outset by Baron Bernstorff, this foreign clique started off wielding great power and, like their master, they were mindful of Hanover's interests in exercising it. It did not take the English ministers long to work this out. The problem was how to counteract it. One approach was to try and win over the German advisers themselves and to neutralise their policies by affability and compromise. This was tried (as when ministers, weak after the abortive attempt to pass a Peerage Bill in 1719, met Bernstorff and his friends) but with limited success. Another tactic was to use the female favourites as a means of putting forward another, more British, point of view directly into the King's private ear. This was to prove more rewarding.

The tangled politics of the first part of the reign can more easily be deciphered by following the tortuous path to power of Viscount Townshend and his brother-in-law Sir Robert

Walpole. A number of early mistakes, in, for example, failing to pay sufficient attention to either the male or the female Germans, cost these English politicians dear. A matter of considerable importance in these years was the desire of Schulenburg for a British title. Townshend did not appreciate the significance of this and deeply offended her by attempting to fob her off with an Irish peerage as Duchess of Munster. Thereafter, as Sir Robert expressed it, she worked for their removal from office 'with more than ordinary zeal and resentment against us'. It is true that in their decline from grace Townshend's lack of enthusiasm for Hanoverian interests was undoubtedly the most important factor in the King's mind, but the animosity of the new Irish duchess added fuel to the fire. The Earl of Sunderland, who managed to ingratiate himself with both the court ladies, did not fall into the same trap, and soon the Duchess of Munster emerged as a fully-fledged swan, Duchess of Kendal in the peerage of Great Britain.

Sunderland's approach proved to be the right one. Though for long also confided in by the German advisers, the Duchess of Kendal evolved as a key agent of the British ministers in their battle to overcome the pernicious influence those Germans exercised over the King. The crunch came in 1720 when, so the ministers heard, the Germans were minded to use their influence to bring in Whigs more sympathetic to the Hanoverian cause. Before long ministerial relations with Townshend and Walpole were patched up and it was arranged they re-join the ministry. The new alliance effectively brought to an end the importance of the male Germans in British politics. It paved the way too for the emergence of Walpole as the King's leading minister in domestic affairs.

There was no greater realist in politics than this earthy country gentleman who kept his own mistress. From the outset of his long period in office he fully recognised the need to ensure that the Duchess of Kendal remained in his camp. When it came to persuading George I to agree to unpalatable policies, Walpole on his own admission 'did everything by her'. Though her political sense was limited she was, in his opinion, 'as much Queen of England as ever any was'. Walpole also knew that she never really liked him and that, in spite of the piety she affected, her support had its price.

Charles II.

Lucy Walter, 'This beautiful strumpet . . . brown, beautiful, bold'.

James Duke of Monmouth, 'darling of his father and the ladies'.

Queen Catherine of
Braganza – she found
tolerance paid.

Nell Gwyn – 'Odds
fish, what company
am I got into?'

Louise de Keroualle.
'I have always loved
her and I die loving
her.'

Lady Castlemaine,
'Most enormously
vicious and ravenous'.

Anne Hyde, Duchess of York. For consolation she became 'one of the highest feeders in England'.

Lady Denham. 'She bestows her favours left and right.'

James II. 'He will lose his soul for a lot of trollops.'

Catherine Sedley. 'It cannot be my beauty . . .'

Ehrengarde Duchess of Kendal 'would have sold the King's honour for a shilling'.

George I. Observers thought he showed bad taste and a strong stomach.

'Solomon in his glory' – the lampoonist's view of George II's new 'German whore', later Lady Yarmouth, replacing his recently-dead Queen.

Queen Caroline of Anspach. 'A handsome creature with a magnificent bosom.'

Few were more grasping than she. She was insatiable for pensions, offices of profit under the Crown, for jewels and outright grants of money. Walpole was heard to complain that she was so venal that she would have sold the King's honour for a shilling advance to the highest bidder. But when he grumbled to the King about rapacious Germans regarding England as the land of promise George merely smiled and suggested 'I suppose you are also paid for your recommendations'. The King had himself given her a Hanoverian pension of £7500 a year but was still keen to see her well provided for in her adopted country.

One particular provision was a source of great embarrassment in the early years of the new ministry. This was the grant to her of a concession to mint coins for Ireland. She sold the patent for a £10,000 profit to a Birmingham manufacturer named Wood. Walpole felt sure there would be a public outcry but, still feeling insecure in office, he was primarily concerned not to hurt the Duchess's feelings and did not call a halt to the proceedings. The result was that the coins Wood produced caused a violent outburst in Ireland, sparked off by Dean Swift who, in his *Drapier's Letters*, was not slow to draw attention to the Duchess's financial involvement.

The ministry was badly mauled but it survived. Yet even such forbearance regarding the Duchess was no guarantee of her loyalty. This Walpole discovered when Bolingbroke, Queen Anne's Tory minister who had later joined the exiled Stuarts, tried to make his peace with the Hanoverian dynasty. Bolingbroke's French wife, a niece of Madame de Maintenon, was clever enough to see that a sure way to bring her husband's case to George I's attention was through the Duchess of Kendal. Bolingbroke, recollecting Lady Masham's usefulness, needed little convincing. In consequence, with the help of a massive bribe (£11,000 was quoted), Lady Bolingbroke made great play of flattering the Duchess and her daughter. The Duchess in turn became enthusiastic about reversing Bolingbroke's attainder and restoring all his rights. Where Jacobite sympathies were concerned, though, special care was required, as the Duchess had discovered after the 1715 Rebellion. When Charles II's grandson, the young Earl of Derwentwater, stood condemned to death for taking part in the uprising it was rumoured that she had been offered a huge sum of money to persuade the King to reprieve him. Such however were the dangers on that occasion, involving the very existence of the Hanoverian succession itself, that it would have been foolish of her to try.

In Bolingbroke's case, George was ready to listen and to accept as genuine the repentant sinner's expressed desire to support the new dynasty. Walpole, though willing to bend to the Duchess to the extent of restoring Bolingbroke's estates, jibbed at the restoration of full political rights, knowing that he would be making a rod for his own back. It was Walpole's view that won the day. Even so he lived to regret even this limited concession, since Bolingbroke, sour and dissatisfied, was soon in active opposition. Equally frustrated, the Duchess continued her intrigues on Bolingbroke's behalf to the end of the reign. Even a ministerial attempt to buy her off with a pension could not deter her. The affair caused Walpole grave concern for his own position, though in the event the cautious King was wise enough to remain loyal to his minister.

The power that the Duchess of Kendal wielded was a source of great annoyance to her more intelligent but less successful rival Kielmannsegg. Therefore when the Duchess was weaned to the English party Kielmannsegg threw her hand in (ineffectively as it turned out) with the Germans. Carteret, when Townshend's fellow Secretary of State, was known to cultivate her in his anti-Townshend and anti-Walpole intrigues, but again to little effect. There were rumours that she also maintained friendly relations with the Prince of Wales after he had quarrelled with his father. The French Ambassador, who was as much concerned with such matters as his predecessors had been a generation before at the court of Charles II, was certainly told that this was so. Actually there was little love lost between her and the Waleses. The sharp-tongued Princess got in some cruel barbs about this royal favourite, one of them drawing attention to the lavishness with which she painted her face: 'She looks young, if one may judge by her complexion, not more than eighteen or twenty.' 'Aye, Madam,' capped Lord Chesterfield, 'eighteen or twenty stone.' It was clear too that the Princess had the painted lady well weighed up when she asserted 'she never stuck a pin in her gown without a design'.

Some of Kielmannsegg's more ridiculous aspects did little

to help her cause, as when, some reflection having been made on her morals, she induced her husband to provide her with a certificate stating 'she had always been a faithful wife'. (How he could prove this is not clear.) But she was shrewder than her more successful rival and, while recognising the limits of her power, she knew the right price to charge for what influence she did have. A man for whom she had obtained an office of profit, for example, had to pay £500 down and then £200 a year. 'And,' added the observant Lady Cowper, 'I have since learned that he gave her also the fine brilliant ear-rings which she wears, it being certain she never had any such jewels abroad.'

Sometimes those anxious not to lose out tried to make sure of their cause by bribing both women. On one occasion they both received £15,000 worth of South Sea Company stock in an endeavour to bring influence to bear on the King in the Company's favour. Another time there was £10,000 each for them when the Duke of Chandos achieved his much-sought-after advancement in the peerage. With such women at work jobbery remained an entrenched part of British political life.

Normally the Countess Platen's influence was limited to Hanover during the King's regular sojourns there, but on one occasion, at the beginning of Walpole's long run in office, she played a role which had important repercussions on the English scene. This was the time when George was accompanied on his electoral visit by the ambitious Carteret whom Walpole had good reason not to trust. By actively supporting pro-Hanoverian foreign policies and by bringing the Countess Platen to his aid, Carteret hoped so to ingratiate himself with the King that his policies would triumph over those of his colleagues. Townshend, the other Secretary of State, having learned his lesson earlier, continued to rely on the good offices of the Duchess of Kendal, taking care both to line her pocket and to fan her jealousy of her old enemy Platen.

In the end miscalculation of Russia's intentions revealed to the King the folly of Carteret's ideas. His fall from grace was accelerated by another wrong-headed plan again involving the Countess, and once more intended to curry favour with the King. The Countess's daughter (possibly by the King – certainly he provided the dowry) was to marry into a French family and Carteret took it upon himself to arrange for the

Regent Orleans to confer on the bridegroom the coveted title of a French duke. Instead of being immediately accommodating the French, to George's enormous embarrassment, began quibbling. It was not long before Carteret was effectively removed from power and Walpole left fully in control.

In the later years of the reign, politics were somewhat more settled and the King's life less troubled. Kielmannsegg too had her reward. With her husband decently dead, she was created first of all Countess of Leinster in the peerage of Ireland and later Countess of Darlington in the British peerage. She never did rise as high as the Duchess. What is more, though the youngest of this strange *ménage à trois*, she had the misfortune to die first. George was then in his mid-sixties. He still had an eye for the ladies and, in the opinion of some, was not above replenishing his harem. Earlier in the reign, though he had not taken the opportunity of obtaining at least some popularity by taking an English mistress, it had been a cause of consolation to some that he had not entirely ignored native talent. True, the Duchess of Shrewsbury, with whom he had ventured certain familiarities soon after his arrival, had been of Italian origin, but he was also seen to admire the Duchess of Bolton, Lady Mary Wortley Montagu (even though smallpox had ruined her looks and she had to rely on personality to attract attention) and Lady Cowper. In later years his supposed attentions to Lord Hervey's young wife had led to aristocratic gossip. Now in his old age he was thought to be attracted by the Countess of Macclesfield's daughter, Anne Brett. Says Horace Walpole, Sir Robert's son, 'Miss Brett had an apartment given her in St. James's Palace, and was to have been created a Countess'.

If so, fate intervened before the King could act. Shortly after Kielmannsegg's death his former wife Sophia Dorothea also passed away, freed at last from her prison. As if to show his lasting contempt George went to the theatre with the Duchess of Kendal the same day that he heard the news. But if good feeling was not among his most notable attributes, superstition certainly was, and it had been foretold that within a year of his wife's death he would follow her to the grave. Sure enough, seven months later, during a last attempt to reach Hanover, he collapsed and died. Perhaps after all Sophia Dorothea had had the last word.

There is a final bizarre postscript to the life of this strange King. If he had been superstitious, the Duchess of Kendal who survived him was even more so, and she spent the rest of her life with the most weird companion. Horace Walpole tells the story:

> George I told the Duchess of Kendal that if he could he would appear to her after his death. Soon after that event a large bird, I forget of what sort, flew into her window. She believed it was the King's soul and took the utmost care of it.

George II

The Right Sow By The Ear

A strange phenomenon, remarked on at the time, was that George II should have a mistress at all, since he had married young and never fell out of love with his wife. His marriage to Princess Caroline of Anspach had been a conventionally political one, but turned out to be supremely successful. Caroline was a handsome creature with a magnificent bosom, and as far as her husband was concerned her physical attractions never palled. In addition she possessed a clear brain, far superior to his though he never knew it. For despite her ambitions she had the good sense to realise that if she were to succeed in life her husband needed the most tactful management. George was an obstinate little man subject to towering rages which might end up with his kicking his wig around the room. And like as not his tantrums, accompanied by cries of 'Stuff' and 'Pooh', would be caused by the merest trifles – because, as his daughter put it, 'one of his pages has powdered his periwig ill, or because a housemaid has set a chair where it does not use to stand'.

It was the supreme achievement of Caroline that she managed to govern this stubborn and irascible prince without his ever realising it, so that when she died he was mournfully to declare 'I never yet saw the woman worthy to buckle her shoe'. In her success her physical attractions played their part. Even in middle age whenever husband and wife met after being separated for any length of time George, after a perfunctory greeting in front of the court, would rush her off to their private apartments. It was his habit to retire to bed with her every afternoon, and indeed it was from one of these siestas that Sir Robert Walpole called him, half-dressed and in his usual state of irritation, to inform him of his father's death and his own accession as King George II.

Why then did this uxorious man find it necessary to take a mistress? Primarily, it would seem, because it was the fashion of the day for princes to do so. Lord Hervey, who as Vice-Chamberlain of the Royal Household had opportunity to study the court pretty closely, probably hit the nail on the head when he observed: 'Though he was incapable of being attached to any woman but his wife, he seemed to look upon a mistress rather as a necessary appurtenance to his grandeur as a Prince than an addition to his pleasure'. Horace Walpole agreed: 'His passions were Germany, the Army and women. Both the latter had a mixture of parade about them.'

The parade had become evident soon after George, as Prince of Wales, had arrived in England with his father. In the time-honoured tradition he singled out for his attentions one of his wife's Maids of Honour. His choice was the Honourable Mary Bellenden and by all accounts of her appearance and character he could scarcely have done better. But it did not take Miss Bellenden long to discover what a lack-lustre lover this German prince was, how lacking in ardour, how tight-fisted, how closely tied to his wife's apron strings. As Lord Hervey wrote: 'Though incontestably the most agreeable, the most insinuating and most likeable woman of her time, made up of every ingredient likely to attach a lover, she began to find out that her situation was only the scandal of being the Prince's mistress without the pleasure, the confinement without the profit.'

In consequence Miss Bellenden cast her eyes about for a more permanent and rewarding candidate for her affections, and gradually extricated herself from her predicament. Luckily there was a substitute mistress waiting in the wings, Henrietta Howard, later Countess of Suffolk. Unlike her predecessor, Mrs Howard, though a woman of taste and discernment, had little room to manoeuvre and a greater need to retain royal favour. She had been involved with the new Royal Family since the days of Queen Anne when the Howards had made their way towards the rising sun of

Hanover. Her husband was both difficult and impecunious, and at that time they could not afford to live in England. After the Hanoverian succession Mrs Howard was taken into Caroline's Household, attending her in the relatively lowly post of bedchamber woman, a position she retained after George made her his mistress. For twenty years she stuck to her unenviable twin tasks of trying to please royal husband and wife, though during the last few years, after her own husband had succeeded as Earl of Suffolk, she was Mistress of the Robes.

Initially it was her husband – 'wrong-headed, ill-tempered, obstinate, drunken, extravagant' in Hervey's view – who was her greatest trial. He was intensely jealous, on one occasion even getting into a fierce argument with Caroline and threatening to drag his erring wife out of her coach. Eventually a pension of £12,000 a year calmed him down. Caroline however used more subtle ways of extracting vengeance on her husband's mistress. Though she affected not to mind, George's infidelity wounded her deeply. Partly to compensate for the degradation she felt she sought in turn to degrade her rival. While calling her 'My good Howard' she would make her perform the most menial tasks. Little titbits were related back to Lord Hervey, as when Caroline insisted Mrs Howard should hold a basin during the ceremony of the Queen's dressing and Mrs Howard 'with her little fierce eyes, and her cheeks as red as your coat' said she would not do it. The Queen replied – 'as I would have said to a naughty child' – 'Yes my dear Howard, I am sure you will'. And she did. To crown all, George himself could be equally cruel, on one occasion snatching the handkerchief his mistress had just tied round his wife's neck, and exclaiming 'Because you have an ugly neck yourself you love to hide the Queen's'.

The time Mrs Howard spent alone with her lover did not made up for such taunts. Though she was no great beauty she was elegant, charming and cultured, but her gifts were largely wasted on George. Not only was his admiration reserved for his wife but he was petty, small-minded and completely lacking in ardour. In his habits he was punctilious to an absurd degree. It was said of him 'He seemed to think his having done a thing today, an unanswerable reason for his doing it tomorrow'. Every evening at exactly the same time he would present himself at his mistress's apartments in the palace. 'He would,' Horace Walpole records, 'frequently walk up and down the gallery of an evening, looking at his watch, for a quarter of an hour before seven, but would not go in till the clock struck.' The three or four hours that followed appear mostly to have been filled with games of cards. So altogether it was not a very romantic relationship which blossomed. Once when the mistress made some complaint to the wife Caroline got another dig in. 'I told her that she and I were not of an age to think of these sorts of things in such a romantic way,' sarcastically adding the admonition 'not to read any romances'. It was not as though there was an abundance of money, either, to make Mrs Howard's life sweeter. Caroline told Lord Hervey that her rival received £2,000 a year before George came to the throne and £3,200 a year afterwards 'besides several little dabs of money'. Compared with his predecessors in England and his contemporaries elsewhere this King spent very little on his extra-marital affairs.

Nor did the lady's position, though she remained in post during the early part of George II's reign, give her anything in the way of power. This remained a period when ministers normally needed the monarch's wholehearted support if they were to continue in office, and when mistresses with access to the monarch could be a useful ally. Yet Sir Robert Walpole, who continued as leading minister, ignored the existence of Mrs Howard. He knew better than anyone that it was the Queen who had the real influence with this king, and that Caroline, in Hervey's words, 'by long studying and long experience of his temper knew how to instill her own sentiments . . . and that whilst she was seemingly on every occasion giving up her opinion and her will to his, she was always in reality turning his opinion and bending his will to hers'. So Walpole 'made use of the alkali of the Queen's temper to sweeten the acid of the King's'. When he boasted in his typically crude fashion that he had taken the right sow by the ear, it was Caroline to whom he referred.

So discreetly did the Queen exercise her control that those outside the King's immediate circle did not know its extent, and many were convinced that, as in previous reigns, the mistress was the power behind the throne. Not only were they backing the wrong horse but Caroline regarded anyone who cultivated the mistress as an enemy to be opposed at all costs. Bolingbroke and others opposed to Walpole did their cause no good by cultivating Mrs Howard. George II's hatred of his father, and the way in which he had given the appearance of being governed by mistresses, automatically put him on his guard. 'That is none of your business, madam,' he was heard to retort to a suggestion of Mrs Howard's, 'you have nothing to do with that.' Still a long list of people including Swift and Pope counted themselves among her friends. They might have been more successful in worldly things had they cultivated a friend of the Queen's rather than the King's. Lady Sundon, for example, was known to be in Caroline's confidence and suspected of taking bribes for advancing office-seekers. A fine pair of earrings came into her possession, it was believed by these means. 'What an impudent creature to come with her bribe in her ear,' stormed the old Duchess of Marlborough after the lady had visited her wearing the offending jewels – to which the quick-witted Lady Mary Wortley Montagu retorted, 'Madam, how should people know where wine is sold, unless a bush is hung out?'

Mrs Howard learned to accept placidly her own lack of power. By irritating the King, says Hervey, 'she had just enough influence, by watching her opportunities, to distress those sometimes to whom she wished ill'. She developed a highly disdainful attitude in rejecting proffered bribes, as when she was promised '*a thousand guineas* to dispose of to whoever is proper' if she obtained someone a post as Lord of the Bedchamber; or told she could lay down her own 'conditions' if she managed to arrange for someone else to be appointed an Equerry. Certainly she could have done with more money when, for instance, she built a modest country villa by the Thames at Twickenham. Here, for once, George appears to have given her a few thousand pounds, but not enough to make the going easy.

With the passage of the years Lady Suffolk, as she now was, became increasingly deaf, and as George was a great talker this did nothing to help her cause. His evening visits became even more of a bore and his treatment of her in public even more peremptory. Her patience at last became exhausted. After twenty years of constant attendance, she took herself off for a few weeks to the fashionable pleasures of Bath, only to find on her return that those increasingly unromantic seven o'clock meetings were not resumed. Horace Walpole was convinced her friendship with Sir Robert's enemy Bolingbroke was a factor involved, but in fact the King seems to have been only too glad to have found an opportunity of bringing an increasingly unpalatable practice to an end.

This final blow to Lady Suffolk's pride could not be kept secret. She therefore took the hint and prepared to depart. Too late Caroline realised the folly of having treated her rival so badly, and the potential dangers involved in her leaving. Was it not probable that another mistress would prove more clever, more malicious and above all more powerful than this one? And who, till that successor emerged, would keep the restless little man happy and fill all those extra evening hours? At the last minute, therefore, the Queen tried to make her old foe think again. She was ticked off by the King for her pains. 'What the devil do you mean by trying to make that old, deaf, peevish beast stay and plague me when I have so good an opportunity of getting rid of her?'

So Lady Suffolk gave up her posts, official and unofficial, and took her leave. By a curious sort of inverted morality, her withdrawal from court led to a public outcry by Walpole's enemies. As Hervey pointed out: 'One would have imagined that the King, instead of dropping a mistress to give himself up entirely to a wife had repudiated some virtuous, obedient, and dutiful wife in order to abandon himself to the dissolute commerce and dangerous sway of some new favourite.' Such was the way of the world in the early eighteenth century. Lady Suffolk did not mind, and was soon reconciled to her lot. She was by now a widow and, as if to cock a snook at her former lover, she soon took a new husband. The man she married was twelve years her junior but she was to outlive him by twenty years, quietly enjoying her villa and the social round.

The wife to whom the King had entirely given himself up now discovered what it meant to have a churlish husband continually at a loose end. One brief interlude taken from life by the Vice-Chamberlain now typified what went on at court.

His majesty stayed about five minutes in the gallery, snubbed the Queen, who was drinking chocolate, for being always stuffing, the Princess Emily for not hearing him, the Princess Caroline for growing fat, the Duke for standing awkwardly, Lord Hervey for not knowing what relation the Prince of Sultzbach was to the Elector Palatine, and then carried the Queen to walk, to be resnubbed in the garden.

He began spending his evenings in his daughters' apartments and took to making eyes at their governess, Lady Deloraine. She was a good-looking woman in her thirties, formerly married to one of the Duke of Monmouth's sons and now to plain Mr Wyndham, the sub-governor of the Duke of Cumberland, the King's younger son. Lady Deloraine happened to be empty-headed, boastful, coquettish, vulgar and inclined to the bottle, in other words the exact opposite of Lady Suffolk. But it was at Lady Deloraine that the King, to everyone's disgust, now set his cap. Even Hervey, whose own morals did not bear examination, was flabbergasted: 'Such was the lady who at present engaged the dalliance of the King's looser hours, his Majesty having chosen not from any violence of passion but as a decent, convenient, natural and unexceptionable commerce, to make the governess of his two youngest daughters his whore and the guardian-director of his son's youth and morals his cuckold.'

From a political point of view Sir Robert Walpole was worried by the potential dangers presented by this new fancy, a woman in his view with 'a weak head, a pretty face, a lying tongue, and a false heart'. In his matter-of-fact way he took the matter up with the Queen, suggesting Lady Tankerville, 'a very safe fool,' as an alternative. 'Send for Lady Tankerville,' he is reported as saying, 'a handsome, good-natured, simple woman (to whom the King had formerly been coquet), out of the country, and place her every evening at commerce or quadrille in the King's way.' His advice appears to have been ignored, or to have had no effect, and Lady Deloraine had no rival.

How far she succumbed to royal pressure is not clear, though it appears that initially she played for time. Later she discussed this most delicate subject with Lady Sundon, whom she hardly knew. 'The King,' she informed her, 'has been very importunate these two years and has often told me how unkind I am to refuse him; that it is mere crossness, or that he is sure my husband would not take it ill.' Walpole, happening to meet her one day carrying a child, quizzed her with his normal lack of inhibition as to whose it was. 'That's a very pretty boy, Lady Deloraine; who got it?' 'Mr Wyndham, upon honour, but I will not promise whose the next shall be.' Later she suggested to Sir Robert that she had not yielded to the royal supplications. 'She was not of an age,' she said plainly enough, 'to act like a vain and loving fool, but if she did consent that she would be well paid; adding, too, that nothing but interest should bribe her, for as to love, she had enough of that, as well as a younger man, at home, and that she thought old men and kings ought always to be made to pay well.' In the end the minister, more concerned with her influence than her morals, happily concluded that this favourite, like the last, would have no power – 'As she only goes to bed with the King, lying *with* him or *to* him is much the same as lying *to* or *with* Mr Wyndham'. For Walpole's money Queen Caroline remained the power behind the throne.

Neither Walpole nor Caroline underrated the importance of the next woman to catch the King's eye even when this happened in far-away Hanover. Normally it was to the great relief of Queen and ministers alike that George, every other year or so, left Caroline in charge while he visited electoral dominions for a few months. Naturally no one expected him to be celibate on these occasions and for many years his needs had been met by Madame d'Elitz. Being, in the Hanoverian tradition, related to another mistress of the Electoral House – the Duchess of Kendal was her aunt – this lady knew well what was expected of her. Indeed it was said of Madame d'Elitz that she gave her favours not only to George II but to his father and to his son as well, hence the quip concerning her – 'There is nothing new under the sun – nor under the grandson either'. Lord Hervey thought her well qualified for such a position, 'a very handsome lady, with a great deal of wit, who had a thousand lovers, and had been catched in bed with a man twenty years ago and been divorced from her husband upon it'.

By this stage Madame d'Elitz was, in the polite parlance of the day, 'a little in decline'. So it was natural that her visiting lover's eyes should wander elsewhere. They came to rest on Amelia Sophia von Walmoden, a pretty woman, just turned thirty, married and described as being 'of the first fashion'. Once again a touch of nepotism crept in since she was the great-niece of that Countess Platen who had been mistress to George's father, and was therefore also a niece of the late unlamented Kielmannsegg. The devotion of the ladies of this family to the intimate needs of the House of Hanover appeared to be limitless.

Though now in his early fifties the King showed a degree of ardour and enthusiasm which had hitherto seemed foreign to his nature or reserved for his more private moments with his wife. In his unselfconscious fashion he bombarded Caroline with letters up to sixty pages long detailing, as Lord Hervey learned, 'every step he took in it, of the growth of his passion, the progress of his applications, and their successes', even giving 'the account of his buying her, which, considering the rank of the purchaser, and the merits of the purchase as he set them forth, I think he had no great reason to brag of, when the first price, according to his report, was only one thousand ducats – a much greater proof of his economy than his passion'.

But passion there undoubtedly was. For weeks the royal return to London was delayed as the King found himself unable to tear himself away. While the British political scene cried out for his presence, the Queen had to manage as best she could without him, assisted only by letters containing such highly presumptuous sentiments as 'I know you will love the Walmoden *because she loves me*'. Anxious as ever to retain her influence over her husband, Caroline did indeed pretend to approve of the liaison, bitterly though she resented and feared it. It was a great relief to her when George eventually returned to London alone. It did not bode well, though, that he brought his lover's portrait with him to hang opposite the foot of his bed. He also had the temerity to suggest to his wife that she arrange a visit of the Princess of Modena to London, as he had heard 'her Highness was pretty free of her person and that he had the greatest inclination imaginable to pay his addresses to a daughter of the late Regent of France'. In the end he had only the ineffectual efforts of Lady Deloraine to divert him and, with his temper in consequence shorter than ever, it was a very miserable winter at the Court of St. James's that year. Caroline pretended not to notice his preoccupation – 'She was sorry for the scandal it gave others, but for herself *she minded it no more than his going to the close stool'*. (After all why should she mind when the worldly Archbishop of York, having discussed the King's new German mistress with Walpole, told her that he 'was glad to find her Majesty so sensible a woman as to like her husband should divert himself '?)

To the consternation of his ministers and the British public it soon became known that, contrary to his usual practice of biennial trips, the King intended to go back to Hanover again the following spring. Too frequent absences of this sort did nothing to help the smooth running of the administration, in which the monarch was still very closely involved, or to ingratiate the new dynasty with the British people whose allegiance, as the 1745 Rebellion a few years later was to show, was not undivided. Stubborn as ever, George would not be deterred and even rushed through the marriage he had arranged for his son, Frederick, Prince of Wales, in order not to delay his return to his new love. In the end, says Hervey, he was in such a state of irritation that 'everyone about him wished him gone almost as much as he wished to leave them'.

He had in fact left Madame Walmoden pregnant and this, in the view of the cynical Hervey, appealed to the vanity of an old man. This child died but another was born later, though in the Hanoverian tradition never officially recognised. He was to be known as Monsieur Louis – a name by which George II appears to have got his own back on his father, for when Caroline had had a son during the late King's reign, George I had refused to allow the name Louis to be used.

On his second visit to Madame Walmoden the King again tarried an unconscionable time in Hanover. Once again in England malicious gossip spread. A broken-down horse, turned loose in the streets of London, was found to bear a notice proclaiming 'Let nobody stop me – I am the King's Hanover equipage going to fetch his Majesty and his whore to England'. 'Lost or strayed out of this house,' read a message found on the door of St. James's Palace, 'a man who has left a wife and six children on the parish; whoever will give any tidings of him to the churchwardens of St. James's Parish, so he may be got again, shall receive four shillings and sixpence reward. N.B. – This reward will not be increased, nobody judging him to deserve a Crown.'

Caroline, though affecting to treat the amour lightly, was at her wits' end. Finally, steeled by Walpole's advice as to what she must do if she was to continue to be a power in the land, she wrote to Hanover suggesting George bring Walmoden to England, assuring him that she would treat her exactly as he would wish. He was deeply touched and as his way of showing it wrote back giving even more details of his liaison. He ordered that Lady Suffolk's old apartments should be prepared. Yet still he dallied in his German dominions, while Englishmen like Lord Hervey began increasingly to fulminate that the British Exchequer was being expected 'to support his Hanover bawdy-houses in magnificence, and enrich his German pimps and whores'.

It was the beginning of the following year before he reappeared – and then without Walmoden. From some sense of discretion, or more probably from a fear of the unknown, she stayed at home. This time the King settled down more easily into his old routine. He made it clear that Caroline remained as high as ever in his affections and re-established the old ritual of card playing in the evenings with Lady Deloraine and the Maids of Honour. As the year wore on it became clear that he did not intend to return to Hanover at the earliest opportunity. Lady Deloraine became quite proud of herself. 'She used to brag of this royal conquest,' says Hervey, 'and say she thought England in general had great obligations to her, and particularly the Administration; for that it was owing to her, and her only, that the King had not gone abroad . . . She used often, after setting forth the violence of the King's passion, and the urgency of his attacks, to ask the Princess Caroline's advice what she should do.' Princess Caroline was one of the King's unmarried daughters, but wise enough in the ways of the world to tell her governess to look elsewhere for advice. Walpole did not mind too much: 'He was not sorry the King had got a new plaything but wished His Majesty had taken someone less mischievous than that lying bitch'. The important thing was that the real influence remained with the Queen.

Now, for King and ministers alike, a catastrophe occurred. The Queen had been ill for some time, but because the King was as intolerant of illness as he was of most things she had endeavoured to hide the fact. The result was fatal. As she lay on her deathbed George was prostrate with a combination of grief and self-pity. Realising his future predicament Caroline advised him to marry again. Lord Hervey could hardly believe his ears when he heard the response this suggestion provoked. 'Wiping his eyes, and sobbing between every word, with much ado he got out his answer: "*Non – j'aurai – des maîtresses*".' To which his long-suffering wife merely replied: '*Ah! mon Dieu! cela n'empêche pas.*' Their whole relationship was summed up in that brief encounter. It was to be encapsulated again when George assured his courtiers: 'He could have been happy with no other woman upon earth for a wife, and that if she had not been his wife, he would rather have had her for his mistress than any other woman he had ever been acquainted with.'

Throughout all this drama Sir Robert Walpole remained filled with gloom and apprehension. As he told Lord Hervey,

> If this woman should die, what a scene of confusion there will be here! Who can tell into what hands the King will fall? Or who will have the management of him? You do not know how often he refuses to hear me when it is on a subject he does not like; but by the Queen I can with time fetch him round to those subjects again; she can make him do things in another shape, and when I give her her lesson, can make him propose the very thing as his own opinion which a week before he had rejected as mine.

The Queen did die and the question of the future management of the King presented itself as a stark reality. Some ministers, the Duke of Newcastle among them, thought that Princess Emily would perhaps inherit her mother's role. The Princess, who was no great friend of Walpole, would not perhaps have been averse to the idea of wielding political power. Walpole had good reason for pooh-poohing the suggestion. 'Does the Princess Emily design to commit incest?' he asked, 'Will she go to bed with her father? or does he desire she should? If not, do not tell me the King intends to make a vow of chastity or that those that lie with him won't have the best interest in him.'

So who the mistress was to be became the most important political question of the hour. It was Walpole who came up with the correct answer:

> I am for Madame Walmoden. I will bring her over and
> I'll have nothing to do with your girls. I was for the wife
> against the mistress, but I will be for the mistress against
> the daughter unless you think the daughter intends to
> behave so as to supply the place of both wife and
> mistress, which, as I have told you before, I know not
> how she can do but by going to bed with him.

The King's principal minister therefore advised his grieving
monarch to send to Hanover immediately. His advice fell on
fruitful ground. In the short interregnum before Madame
Walmoden arrived Walpole, acting on the principle that
'people must wear old gloves till they could get new ones', was
brazen enough to advise the King's daughters to 'bring my
Lady Deloraine to their father for the sake of his health'. The
father however did not need such assistance. Though he
complained that the governess stank of Spanish wine he
continued, much to Hervey's disgust, to see her as before,
'without the least alteration in his manner of talking to her or
his manner of paying her, and in short sent for this old
acquaintance to his apartment for just the same motives that
people send casually for a new one to a tavern'.

Madame Walmoden eventually arrived. Initially she
brought her long-suffering husband with her, but in a year or
two she returned temporarily to Hanover and divorced him.
(George accompanied her, having piously informed his Privy
Council 'We have determined, by the blessing of God, for
diverse weighty reasons speedily to go in person beyond the
seas'.) On her return she was created Countess of Yarmouth
and a relatively settled domesticity descended on the scene for
the remaining twenty years of the King's life. In each of the
royal palaces she had her apartments where George, clock-like
as ever, visited her each day – and where his ministers also
came to pay their respects and seek her goodwill.

Her years in England corresponded closely with those when
Madame de Pompadour reigned at Versailles as mistress of
Louis XV, but with vastly different results. Whereas, for
example, Madame de Pompadour, with the generous assistance of her royal lover, accumulated estates and houses,
collected jewels and had money to spend almost at will, Lady
Yarmouth's material gains were insignificant. Nor were they
in the same league when it came to exercising power. Writing

from London, with all the contempt of a representative of an absolute monarchy for a country where Parliament exercised a certain influence over events, the Comte de Gisors suggested that 'Whereas Madame de Pompadour shares the absolute power of Louis XV, Lady Yarmouth shares the absolute impotence of George II'. This was a distortion of the truth. George II was very far from being impotent politically. He continued however to deplore the fact that his father had given the appearance of being governed by mistresses and he consciously endeavoured to avoid falling into the same trap. So Lady Yarmouth never matched Queen Caroline in political importance, and certainly never exercised the same degree of control over domestic and foreign affairs that Madame de Pompadour exercised in France. By the same token, she never became the scapegoat that Pompadour became when affairs went badly for her country and its monarch. Tactful and discreet, Lady Yarmouth kept herself out of the public eye. Whatever influence she acquired was exercised behind closed doors. But in any case it was in her character to be primarily a soother, one who made smooth the rough places for others to walk along.

In her early years in England her importance, except for keeping more dangerous women at bay, appears to have been small. Once, in requesting one of the ministers to procure some place of minor importance for one of her servants, she insisted that he should not tell the King 'because if it be known that I have applied, I have no chance of succeeding'. 'Lady Yarmouth,' concluded Horace Walpole, 'was inoffensive and attentive only to pleasing him and to selling Peerages whenever she had an opportunity.' The story is that early on, being in some financial difficulty, she asked the King for £30,000 which he characteristically refused to give. However he did compromise to the extent of allowing her to nominate two candidates acceptable to Sir Robert Walpole for elevation to the peerage with a fee from each to be payable to her. Walpole was agreeable, two candidates were found, Lady Yarmouth got her money and the King was well satisfied that the whole business had not cost him a penny.

Walpole's ministry was followed, after a brief interlude, by another relatively stable one under Henry Pelham. It was Pelham's death in 1754, six years before the King's, which

91

ushered in a period of political uncertainty when, with leading politicians vying with one another for the King's support, Lady Yarmouth came to assume a role of some significance. Having hitherto acted merely as the confidante to whom ministers paid court, carrying their messages to the monarch and helping them to approach him in the least irritating manner, she was now from time to time made use of in the process of making and retaining ministers. Initially, in order to bolster up Pelham's successor, the Duke of Newcastle, Henry Fox was brought in as Secretary of State with Lady Yarmouth acting as an intermediary. This arrangement did not last. Before long Fox, having decided to quit, poured out his complaints to her, comparing Newcastle's duplicity with Walpole's straightforwardness. 'Ah! Monsieur Fox,' she is said to have replied, 'il y avait bien de la différence entre ces deux hommes là!' But all her entreaties on the King's behalf could not persuade Fox to stay in office – whereupon she asked someone else to convey Fox's explanations to her lover.

Fox's departure paved the way for the elder Pitt, whose anti-Hanoverian speeches had made him George II's bête noire. But now Pitt was anxious to be conciliatory, and in considering how to proceed took to heart Lord Chesterfield's view of George II's relationship with this mistress of long standing: 'Even the wisest man, like the chameleon, takes on without knowing it more or less the hue of what he is often upon.' In consequence the Pages of the back-stairs at St. James's Palace were early one morning rushing about calling 'Mr Pitt wants to see my Lady Yarmouth'. The Great Commoner had come to explain himself in the best way he knew to ensure that his words reached his Sovereign's ear in a sympathetic manner.

Though Pitt came into office the King was furious at the way in which his mistress had been used. 'Mr Pitt shall not go to that channel any more. She does not meddle and shall not meddle.' Even so the channel continued to be used. Pitt himself found the lady a useful ally, and when the King appeared to be turning against him she plucked up courage and warned George that, the political groupings in the House of Commons being then what they were, he had little alternative but to keep him. 'He was angry with her to a degree that stopped her mouth,' reported Newcastle, 'but I hope I have opened it again.' Certainly no one made greater use of the mistress than the timid and neurotic Duke who shared office with Pitt for the last three years of the reign. 'I know you have been tormenting Lady Yarmouth about it,' was one of the old King's *cris de coeur*, 'Why do you plague her? What has she to do with these things? The only comfortable two hours I have in the whole day are those I pass there and you are always teasing her about these things.'

Still the teasing went on, with the lady playing a role almost equivalent to a modern monarch's private secretary, until the irritable old man died at the age of seventy-seven. Rarely can a mistress, carefully pouring oil on troubled waters, have been such an influence for good. Lady Yarmouth is one of the unsung, and almost unknown, heroines of British history.

She had done perhaps one disservice to the throne, for her presence had provided an additional excuse for the King's grandson and heir, the future George III, to remain aloof from the court in the King's old age on the grounds of his grandfather's immorality. This was ironical for the Hanoverian tradition of keeping mistresses had been passed on in full measure to George II's son and George III's father, Frederick Prince of Wales. He had come to England when he was twenty-one, having already savoured the delights of Madame d'Elitz, and by the time he was twenty-four it had been noted 'he has had several mistresses and now keeps one, an apothecary's daughter of Kingston, but is not nice in his choice, and talks more of his feats this way than he acts'. 'Like the rest of his race,' Horace Walpole had pointed out, 'beauty was not a necessary ingredient.' Soon Frederick had followed precedent in living with one of his mother's Maids of Honour, Anne Vane, who bore him a son. Her other lover was Lord Hervey and it had proved a most scandalous and acrimonious affair even by Hanoverian standards.

Eventually a dynastic marriage had been arranged for him with a seventeen-year-old German princess and, though Queen Caroline characteristically advised her daughter-in-law to be 'easy in regard to amours', Frederick in fact settled down to enjoy married bliss. In consequence the future George III spent his childhood in a home where domesticity was prized. The foundations of this home life were shaken by the premature death of Frederick – to be known to posterity as 'Poor

Fred' – but the Princess of Wales had afterwards drawn on the help of her husband's friend, the Earl of Bute, to assist in the upbringing of her son. Though Bute was accused of being the Princess's lover, he was in fact a puritan whose narrow views had a profound effect on the future George III. With his grandfather's mode of living pointed out to him as highly reprehensible this George somewhat priggishly kept himself at arm's length, and determined that he would never take a mistress. So it was that when he came to the throne at the age of twenty-two, while Lady Yarmouth was preparing her return to Hanover with the strong-box said to contain £10,000 left to her by George II, the first proclamation of the new reign was a denunciation of immorality.

George III's moral fight was to be no easy one for he was highly susceptible to female beauty. He spent his youth trying to avoid Cupid's darts and the rest of his life waging war against the sins of the flesh. The tale of his having an affair with the fair Quakeress Hannah Lightfoot is a fairy story (perhaps he cast sheep's eyes at her when passing) but in the early months of his reign his heart almost overcame his head when it came to resisting the beauty and charm of Lady Sarah Lennox, a descendant of Charles II and the Duchess of Portsmouth. Had he given way it would have been to marry her. Instead he hastened to do his dynastic duty in marrying a suitable German princess. Though his bride, Queen Charlotte, had admirable qualities, she was decidedly plain with an ugly nose and mouth and was much given to taking snuff. Determined to show those moral qualities so lacking in his predecessors George III set out to prove a model of fidelity, fathering fifteen children on his wife over the next twenty years. Even so he had difficulty in 'keeping under', to use his own words, his sensual feelings. They were never eradicated and were apt to break out during his later bouts of mental derangement, as when he wrote love letters to Lady Pembroke, and when, at the age of seventy-three, he told his Prime Minister that he intended to go and live in Hanover with a lady of his liking.

Still he took the utmost care to ensure that his children, and most specially his own heir, should follow the example of good living he, in contrast to his grandfather, had set them. Alas, he was to spend most of his life reaping the whirlwind.

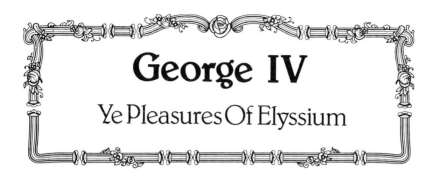

George IV
Ye Pleasures Of Elyssium

It was George III's endeavour to raise his seven sons who grew to manhood in such a manner as to send them into the world immune to temptation. Unfortunately he possessed the disastrous failing that befalls some parents – he was close to his sons when they were small but unable to communicate with them as they grew up. In no case was this more pronounced than with his first-born, George, Prince of Wales. Perhaps as a result of this paternal failure the Prince developed into a remarkable combination of virtue and vices: he could be both the most solicitous and the most incorrigible of sons, at once the most devoted and the most unreliable of friends, at times the most refined and then the most degraded of men. His restrictive upbringing and education were a disaster, designed to repress the irrepressible, chain down an uncontrollable *joie de vivre*, and to keep on ice the hot blood of a youth who knew that one day the world would be at his feet.

The over-regulated life and the detached fatherly moralising had precisely the opposite effect from that intended. Already when he was in his middle teens, a handsome and intelligent youth, the Prince was yearning for the attractions he saw outside the palace walls. Even at this stage, while still officially under the close supervision of his parents, one of Queen Charlotte's ladies discovered that some of his associates had introduced 'improper company' into his rooms when he was supposed to be in bed. From an early age he began developing violent passions for attractive women, laying siege when he was only sixteen to one of his sisters' attendants, Mary Hamilton. Already he displayed what was to prove a life-long weakness for pouring out his love in long, adoring letters. Respectable Mary Hamilton held him at bay. Luckily for her he was only seventeen when he fell in love again, with someone far less worthy. This was the actress Mary Robinson whom he saw as Perdita in *A Winter's Tale*. Immediately he commenced a barrage of highly-charged letters addressed to 'Perdita' and signed 'Florizel'. Mrs Robinson was twenty-one and of dubious repute. As she had already been imprisoned with her husband for debt, she could not but count this royal infatuation as a piece of the greatest good fortune and something to be encouraged. But before long (and again setting a pattern) George's passion began to wane, only for him to find that an affair of the heart is not as easily dropped as it has been taken up. Perhaps because he had a strong streak of duplicity in his character he never in his life learned the art of terminating such relationships amicably. The scorned Perdita still had his compromising letters and she threatened to publish them. King George III, shocked that his son in spite of all parental endeavours had got into such a 'shameful scrape' at such an early age, was obliged to pay £5,000 to get the dangerous missives back. To this the Prince had privately to add a considerable sum before he was rid of what he now termed 'ye old infernal cause Robinson'.

The young Prince of Wales had discovered very early in life that passion could soon lead to pain. But in spite of such experiences he proved unwilling or unable to control himself. Even his Equerry's suggestion that he learn a lesson from the Robinson affair and stop writing compromising love letters to 'a certain sort of ladies' had no effect. Nor did his father get anywhere by pointing out to him, when he was only eighteen, 'your love of dissipation has for some months been with enough ill-nature trumpeted in the papers'. To the Prince his father was merely being 'excessively cross and ill-tempered and uncommonly grumpy'. So for half a century his dissipation was to be trumpeted in like manner together, in the course of time, with the dissipation of his younger brothers. Small wonder that in the end the Duke of Wellington was moved to call them 'the damnedest millstone about the necks of any Government that can be imagined'. The good effect on the minds of the British people of the sober and respectable habits of George III and Queen Charlotte was almost completely annihilated by the fast living and over-indulgence of their sons, led by the eldest.

There was no interruption in the Prince of Wales's love affairs. Among those he fell for was Lady Melbourne (though her son, the future Prime Minister, was reckoned to have been Lord Egremont's and not the Prince's). He was already showing a weakness for mature women which was to grow with the years, reflecting perhaps both a need for a mother-figure and a deep-seated desire for domesticity. At this stage, however, he more often found satisfaction with younger women who had little reputation left to lose. Sometimes, it appears, offspring resulted – one accommodating woman he made a mother adopted the feminine forms of his names, Georgiana Augusta Frederica, in order to pin the paternity of her daughter firmly on her royal lover.

Perhaps the most embarrassing escapade of the Prince's early life happened, when he was only eighteen, with the 'divinely pretty' Madame von Hardenburg, wife of a Hanoverian diplomat. As George told his next-eldest brother, Frederick, Duke of York, she first caught his eye while playing cards in his mother's apartments. Immediately 'ye fatal tho' delightful passion arose in my bosom,' so that he 'dropped every other connexion of whatever sort or kind, and devoted myself entirely to this angelick little woman'. He made himself ill with desire and found that this excited the lady's pity. (It was a device he was to use frequently in future.) In the end he was pleased to report 'I enjoyed ye pleasures of Elyssium'. Unfortunately the irate husband got wind of the affair and Madame von Hardenburg caused considerable embarrassment by writing to her young lover 'saying she hoped I had not forgot all my vows, and would run off with her that night'. In his dilemma the young man confessed everything to his mother. Eventually the King sent the Hardenburgs packing. Afterwards Hardenburg, finding that the scandal had undermined his position, resigned from the Hanoverian service. In consequence it was as a statesman of Prussia that he came to play an important role later in the struggle against Napoleon.

So it was that the Prince of Wales was launched on a fast life even before he left the care of his prudish parents. On his coming of age, by now an extremely handsome and polished young man, with his own home at Carlton House and an increased income, he seemed marked out for a wild existence. His own description of himself was someone 'rather fond of wine and women'. This was a gross understatement. Alongside his sexual appetite and his excessive eating and drinking went an extravagance exacerbated by his gambling, a taste for large-scale building operations and his habit of collecting on a truly colossal scale, all of which led him into perpetual trouble. To make matters worse, in his father's eyes, was his early friendship with Charles Fox, one of the leading opponents of the King's ministers. This was partly the traditional wooing of the heir to the throne by opposition politicians. But in Fox's case the politician's loose morals and fast way of life were an additional attraction to this heir. Though Fox did not lead his protegé anywhere he did not wish to go, nevertheless their relationship increased George III's hatred of Fox to a point where it was virtually insurmountable.

Another influence on the young Prince's life which his father had good reason to suspect was that of the King's own brothers. The Dukes of Gloucester and Cumberland lived their lives with none of George III's inhibitions. Both in their day had been dissipated men-about-town whose habits the Prince of Wales was more willing to acquire than those of his own father. Furthermore, they had both contracted secret marriages with ladies of somewhat murky background. It was as a direct result of their actions in contracting what the King regarded as scandalous marriages that, at George III's request, the Royal Marriages Act of 1772 had been passed. Henceforward it became necessary for a member of the Royal Family seeking to marry to ask for the Sovereign's consent in the first instance; there was then a procedure for seeking parliamentary approval. It was with his own sons' future in the forefront of his mind that George III obtained this power. He could not have realised that its effect would sometimes be little short of disastrous. The suggestion made in the House of Commons that the title of the Act needed to be changed to 'An Act for enlarging and extending the prerogative of the Crown, and for encouragement of adultery and fornication under the pretence of regulating the Marriages of the Royal Family' was to prove not too wide of the mark.

The Prince of Wales came up against its terms very early in his career. It was when he was twenty-one that he met a woman with whom he felt sure he could have a deeper, more permanent relationship than he had hitherto experienced. The object of his affections was six years older than himself. Her name was Maria Fitzherbert, and in some ways she was eminently suitable. With her long nose and dark features she may have been no beauty, but she had serenity and nobility. From a good family, she also had a gentility, an innate discretion and an air of common sense that universally commanded respect. She was neither loose in her morals nor anxious for money or high position. In other ways she was an absolutely impossible choice for the heir to the throne. Not only was she a commoner twice widowed but she was a Roman Catholic. In addition to the Royal Marriages Act preventing the King's son from marrying without his father's consent, the heir to the throne, under the Act of Settlement of 1701, could not marry a Catholic without depriving himself of his rights of succession.

Mrs Fitzherbert was fully aware of the impossibility of contracting a legal marriage with the Prince of Wales. The Prince's dilemma was that she could not marry him in accordance with the law of the land and was too religious and respectable to become his mistress. Meanwhile he was beside himself with passion. The more she resisted the more frantic he became. She was 'dearer to me than life', and mere threats of suicide having got him nowhere, he stabbed himself to prove his feelings. When she withdrew to the Continent and the King absolutely forbade his son to follow her, he bombarded her with love letters.

This took place at a time when he was being pressed to make a suitable marriage with a foreign princess, not only to produce an heir but also to increase his income to cope with his already enormous debts, and not least to help establish his position in the country. 'Till you marry, sir, and have children,' he was told, 'you have no solid hold on the affections of the people.' 'I will never marry,' came his reply, 'my resolution is taken on that subject.' In other words, his passion for Mrs Fitzherbert at this time prevented him from transacting a suitable dynastic marriage, a marriage which might have prevented so much personal anguish in the future.

For a year and a half Mrs Fitzherbert withstood her lover's attacks. Finally, when it was obvious that this was no passing affection, she succumbed. In December 1785 an Anglican clergyman was procured from a debtors' prison to marry them. Under Canon Law the marriage was valid. Yet no one was more aware than Mrs Fitzherbert that under the law of the land it was invalid, a sham which the Prince of Wales wanted in order to demonstrate his determination to unite himself permanently with his dearest Maria. Mrs Fitzherbert was an honest woman. She admitted years later that, though she was given a signed and witnessed marriage certificate, she had 'given herself up to him, exacted no conditions, trusted to his honour, and set no value on the ceremony he insisted on having solemnised'.

Though Mrs Fitzherbert went on living in her own home, using her old name, and conducting herself with a quiet dignity which no one could fault, the marriage secret was soon guessed at. But though the Prince's devotion to her was obvious, the background to their relationship was not publicly admitted. Indeed, the Prince misled his friend Fox on the subject, and it was to sully Fox's reputation when he denied the marriage in the House of Commons. This denial was followed by a partial settlement by Parliament of the Prince's debts. The respite was temporary, however. Soon the heir to the throne was in dire financial straits once more. As he sunk further and further under his load of debt it became quite apparent that only a dynastic marriage, bringing a substantial rise in income, could help him. His father's first bout of madness underlined the need to assure the succession into the next generation, and the outbreak of the French Revolution demonstrated in a dramatic way the need for the Royal Family to retain its popularity.

Even so the Prince of Wales for long remained incorrigible and, indeed, increasingly resumed his old raffish mode of life. In spite of his continued attachment to Mrs Fitzherbert, he found his emotions were still capable of being raised to ecstatic heights by other ladies, some of aristocratic background, some emanating from the gutter. In particular his affair with the actress Anna Maria Crouch proved that he had learned nothing since the days of Perdita. Not only did this new object of his passion receive jewels and a promissory note for £10,000 but he repeated his former folly of writing highly compromising letters. Once more when passion had cooled there came threats of publication, to be followed by the trouble and expense of retrieving the incriminating evidence.

It required all Mrs Fitzherbert's patience and forgiving nature to enable her to retain her dignity and stand by the Prince through such escapades. When, however, turning thirty and already losing his youthful slimness and good looks, he became enamoured of the stately Countess of Jersey, Maria found her own position completely undermined. Lady Jersey was already turned forty and a grandmother nine times over, yet the Prince of Wales found her fascinating and seductive. Later both he and Lord Jersey, whom he was to make Master of the Horse, were to swear that the royal relationship with Frances was an honourable one. Even if this were so, and despite the fact that she was the daughter of a bishop, Lady Jersey was a scheming woman. It became her ambition to entice her lover away from Mrs Fitzherbert completely. Having failed to do this by direct methods she resorted to devious ones. As George was to admit, it was her advice 'which contributed not a little to decide me to marriage'.

By this stage it was apparent even to the Prince of Wales that King and Parliament would never assist him to diminish his crushing load of debt, now well over half a million pounds, unless he contracted a marriage with a suitable princess. For a long time he postponed taking action, telling his father in 1791, for example, 'that as to us Princes particularly the choice of a wife was indeed a lottery, and one from the wheel of which I did not at least at present intend to draw a ticket'. 'I should never marry,' he declared another time, 'unless at the moment I did I thought I preferr'd the woman I was going to marry to every creature in the world.' In the end, hedged in by debt, his ardour for Mrs Fitzherbert having cooled, and egged on by Lady Jersey, he decided to take the plunge. Having made generous financial arrangements for Mrs Fitzherbert, he put himself at his father's disposal.

George III would probably have allowed his son to marry almost any Protestant princess, though the fact that he had never let him go abroad meant that the prospective bridegroom's knowledge of the field was small. Perhaps the fact that his father had contracted a successful marriage without having first met his wife made the son feel that there was no need to be too particular in his choice. George III had however made careful enquiries before committing himself. The most extraordinary feature of this marriage was that the Prince of Wales, normally most fastidious in personal matters and with definite taste as regards women, should have taken so little trouble in the matter, acting more like a prisoner being led out to execution than a man seeking a partner for life. He felt his father would be best pleased if he married his cousin, Princess Caroline of Brunswick, and, presumably on the basis that one German princess was very like another, gave the matter no further thought. The result was a marriage doomed from the outset.

The first meeting of the unhappy couple was in London immediately prior to their wedding. Caroline was not much taken with the bloated figure of her intended husband, but her reaction was nothing to his. 'Pray get me a glass of brandy' he demanded of an attendant after embracing her. For not only was she overblown, fat and blowsy, but her personal hygiene obviously left much to be desired. In addition Caroline turned out to be coarse and vulgar, without grace, polish or discretion. For someone as particular as the Prince, who prided himself on his manners and who liked his women to be of 'perfect cleanliness and sweetness', it was an unbearable prospect. It was, however, too late.

Weeping and stealing glances at Lady Jersey he managed to get through the wedding ceremony. By dint of further drinking he managed to spend the wedding night in the bridal bedroom, in the fireplace instead of the nuptial bed. The Princess was to prove a most unreliable witness, but if she is to be believed they shared a bed for only two weeks. This proved long enough for him to father a child. Nine months later Caroline was delivered of 'an immense girl' (who, ironically, was to die before her father). George felt he had done his duty.

By this stage he found life with his wife quite intolerable, though the fault did not lie entirely on her side. Having made the initial error of choosing such an unsuitable bride so carelessly, the Prince made little effort to make the best of a bad bargain. He was, for instance, unfeeling enough to insist (in the manner of Charles II with Lady Castlemaine) that the Countess of Jersey be one of his wife's Ladies of the Bedchamber. Not being a passive and submissive creature, Caroline thereafter continually drew attention to the Countess, bluntly calling her the Prince's 'mistress'. George insisted that Lady Jersey was only 'a friend to whom I am attached by strong ties of habitude, esteem and respect' but Caroline persisted in what he called 'irritating insinuations' and pressed for the lady's dismissal. Though eventually, with very bad grace, Lady Jersey resigned, there is little doubt that her relationship with the Prince and Caroline's consequent strictures contributed significantly to the complete breakdown of the marriage, to the extent that the husband refused even to preserve appearances by living in the same house as his wife. The Princess made no secret of her ill-treatment, and her grievances as an injured wife were soon trumpeted in the press, resulting in a dramatic rise in the Prince of Wales's unpopularity in the country. This unpopularity, exacerbated by his subsequent mode of life and his later relationships with other women, led over the years to a substantial undermining of the position of the monarchy.

Caroline's own behaviour was, if anything, worse than her husband's. Denied security and affection in her marriage, she sought them elsewhere, out-playing her husband at his own game. All feminine delicacy was thrown away in the process, and with the passage of time her behaviour became at best bizarre and at worst verging on the insane. During the early years of separation, since Fox and the Whigs supported the husband, Tory politicians were inclined to be sympathetic to the wife. The rising star of the Tory Party, George Canning, was one of those who was attracted to her small court and found favour. Indeed the Prince became convinced that what he called 'extreme intimacy' took place between them. There is no evidence of this (Canning was perhaps saved by his early marriage) but later, when the Prince became Regent and King, these suspicions stunted Canning's career for some years. Certainly the Princess's flamboyant behaviour encouraged people to believe the worst. Some years later, following rumours that she had had another child, a 'Delicate Investigation' into her conduct was officially instituted and, whilst it cleared her of the specific charge, it found her general behaviour highly reprehensible. Her husband was dissatisfied even with this conclusion, and as his Whig associates did not press the issue he came to adopt a cooler attitude towards them. Thus, when he eventually became Regent, he did not, as they expected, immediately dismiss his father's Tory ministers and call his erstwhile friends to power.

It benefited Lady Jersey little when the Prince and Princess of Wales went their separate ways. From the very beginning of his association with the vulgar Princess George recollected the attractions of his old love, that most ladylike of commoners, Maria Fitzherbert. On the day of his marriage he sent her a message: 'Tell Mrs Fitzherbert she is the only woman I shall ever love', and in the will he made a year later he described her as *my wife, the wife of my heart and soul*, and though by the laws of this country she *could not avail herself publicly of that name, still such she is in the eyes of Heaven*. All Lady Jersey's mischief-making on her own account had been of no avail. In dropping Caroline George became equally anxious to drop the Countess, for he knew he must do so if he was to have any chance of returning to the consolations of Mrs Fitzherbert. Unfortunately, like so many others of the Prince's loves, Lady Jersey took umbrage and would not allow herself to be dropped gracefully. Not only did she continue to haunt him on public occasions, but in her anger she became a partisan of the Princess of Wales. 'That infernal Jezebel', as her former lover now termed her, was to be a thorn in his flesh for many years. Even when Caroline eventually returned to claim her position as Queen Lady Jersey was to be found frantically trying to drum up support for her former rival. 'Poor woman,' lamented Madame de Lieven, the Russian Ambassador's wife, 'she is quite frenzied – she ought to go out and cool herself in the rain.'

If Lady Jersey was hard to drop, Mrs Fitzherbert proved even harder to win back. Though, in spite of everything, her love for the Prince remained, she refused to be moved by the torrent of tear-stained missives which again bore down on her. However dubious her status had been before, the official marriage had put her in an even more invidious position. Still the barrage of appeals continued, including even a plea from the Prince's mother. Finally, in desperation, Mrs Fitzherbert appealed to the Pope. It was with his sanction that she eventually agreed to share her life once again with the Prince of Wales. Though in the eyes of the Roman Catholic Church her marriage might remain valid, and though the couple made no attempt to hide the fact that they were together again, she nevertheless made her own far-reaching conditions. 'I did not,' she told a friend, 'consent to make up with the Prince to live with him either as his wife or his mistress.' Instead 'we live like brother and sister'.

Mrs Fitzherbert later described the next eight years as 'the happiest of her connection with the Prince'. She certainly was able, as no one else could, to curb his more headstrong tendencies and his weakness for the bottle. Even so, though a platonic relationship might suit a respectable lady in her mid-forties, for a noted roué some years younger it contained the seeds of discord. For long Mrs Fitzherbert turned a blind eye to the Prince of Wales's occasional affairs. (It is likely that it was one of these which produced a son who, as George in old age was to tell the Lord Chancellor, was 'an officer in the East Indies, to whom he felt himself bound to give a legacy of £30,000'.) It was not however a casual liaison which brought about the final break between the Prince and Mrs Fitzherbert but another grand passion for another *grande dame*.

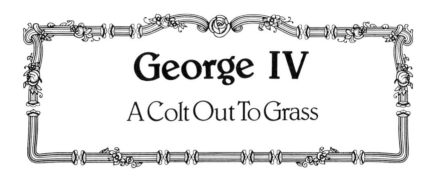

George IV

A Colt Out To Grass

At first sight Isabella Marchioness of Hertford was a most unlikely candidate for the post of a prince's mistress. Perhaps in the strict physical sense she never was. Like some of her predecessors she was a married woman in her late forties, some years older than the Prince of Wales, but with her own strict code of ethics, jealous of her good name and reputation. She was also, in accordance with her lover's taste, handsome, statuesque, matronly. *'Il paraît que vous aimez les vieilles femmes en Angleterre'* was Napoleon's amused reaction when he heard that the heir to Britain's throne had once more succumbed to such overblown charms.

In addition to being a mother figure Lady Hertford provided something else for which the Prince of Wales craved, a happy and stable family life. She had a husband in his sixties, and a number of children, and it was a new-found joy for George to join in the 'perfect tranquillity' of a close-knit family circle. He looked forward eagerly to visits to their country home at 'dear Ragley' and to 'comfortable chats' with 'my best and ever dearest friend'. When they were apart he wrote her long letters with many messages to 'dear Lord Hertford'. Besotted with love, this now grossly fat, dissipated and foolish middle-aged man still allowed his pen to run away with him. 'I really do feel,' he told this new love just before she returned to him in London, 'quite like a young colt going to be turned out to his first grass, as gay as a lark and as light as a feather, and pray tell Lord Hertford (with all that is kindest from me) that

I shall be quite content if you are only half as glad to see me as I shall be rejoiced to see you.'

The plain fact was that Lady Hertford was not half as glad. She was not even a good correspondent, a weakness which was apt to bring her petulant requests from her lover – 'Pray tell me something of your motions, of which I cannot bear to be so long ignorant'. According to Lady Bessborough, George almost made himself ill trying to persuade his Isabella 'to live with him publicly', and indeed on one occasion it was reported that an indignant Lord Hertford had proof 'that HRH has been too *familiar* with her'. But Lady Hertford was a cold fish who continued to do her best not to be hooked. The Prince's frustration was revealed in an onslaught he made on Lady Bessborough, an old flame of his youth. 'He threw himself on his knees,' she wrote afterwards, 'and grasping me round, kissed my neck...he continued sometimes struggling with me, sometimes sobbing and crying...he would break with Mrs F and Ly H, I should *make my own terms*!! I should be his sole confidant, sole adviser – private or public – I should guide his politics.' Though Lady Bessborough, as a friend of Canning, might have found it useful to guide this royal admirer's politics, her reaction to his onslaught was not to know whether to laugh or cry at 'that immense, grotesque figure flouncing half on the couch, half on the ground'. She congratulated herself on managing to keep him at bay.

If Lady Hertford failed to give her lover full satisfaction, she was sufficiently malicious to seek to undermine Mrs Fitzherbert's position by publicly flaunting her hold over the Prince. It was bad enough for Mrs Fitzherbert that the man who had begged her to have him back had gradually dropped his habit of visiting her each evening. Now, as the ascendancy of the new favourite became more obvious, Mrs Fitzherbert had to tell him 'I owe it to myself not to be insulted under your roof with impunity'. Though in his heart of hearts he remained deeply attached to his Maria, Lady Hertford's hold over him was now so great that he made no real effort to prevent a rift. The final break occurred soon after George III finally lost his senses and the Prince of Wales, at the age of forty-eight, became Prince Regent. He sent Mrs Fitzherbert an invitation to a great fête to be held at Carlton House, and she refused to attend on the grounds that he proposed to exclude her from his table. 'I can never submit to appear in your house in any place or situation but that where you yourself first placed me,' she told him as she took herself out of his life for good.

For the remaining nineteen years of the Prince's life he was effectively Head of State. Hitherto he had exercised no power in the country and his mistresses had likewise lacked influence (in contrast to Mrs Clarke, his brother Frederick's mistress, who had caused public scandal by abusing her lover's position as head of the Army and accepting bribes to obtain commissions). From now on the Prince's life and liaisons were scrutinised for evidence of power being exerted by his intimates. When, for instance, the Whig politicians took umbrage at his not dismissing his father's ministers, Lord Grey, the future Prime Minister, denounced Lady Hertford as 'an influence of odious character' which 'lurked behind the throne'. The fact that this lady was related to Lord Castlereagh, a Tory minister much in the forefront of affairs during the next ten years, gave some credence to this belief. Princess Lieven was one of those who was convinced that the Hertford connection put Castlereagh 'on a more intimate footing with his master, and gave him an added power'. Castlereagh would undoubtedly have been a minister with great weight in any case, and though Lady Hertford obtained places for her husband and son in the Regent's Household, her influence was easily exaggerated. Opposition figures were happy to provide the exaggeration. As Lord Holland was later to confess, 'We all encouraged every species of satire against him and his mistress'.

Henry Brougham, the future Whig Lord Chancellor, established his name as counsel for the defence in cases involving George's reputation. The first such case occurred in the early years of the Regency. A suggestion in a poem that the Regent was the 'Adonis of loveliness', a patent absurdity to all but the recipient of the compliment, had provoked Leigh Hunt into publishing a more apt description – 'a violator of his word, a libertine head over heels in debt and disgrace, a despiser of domestic ties, the companion of gamblers and demireps'. Brougham's defence did not prevent Leigh Hunt from serving a prison sentence for his audacity.

By this stage the Prince's reputation with the public was

such that his good points were passed over – his good taste, the breadth of his interests, his patronage of the arts, his personal charm and kindness which won over many, including even Lord Byron. Attention focused on his extravagance and his follies, his relationship with his wife and his increasingly incongruous love affairs. Together with his appearance this provided wonderful material for the lampoonists, whose fierce barbs added to the growing power of the press. Unfortunately for the Prince, he was called upon to head the nation at a time of great turmoil, during the final years of the struggle against Napoleon and the period of depression and repression which followed. In consequence his way of life attracted attention when his countrymen were least willing to tolerate it. However deeply he himself felt the insults, his own behaviour, and not least his sexual peccadilloes, provided the perfect vehicle for undermining the foundations of the monarchy.

In 1820 George III died and, at the age of fifty-seven, the Prince Regent became King George IV. This was the signal for his wife, who had for some years conveniently lived abroad, to return and claim her position as Queen. An immediate crisis resulted. With the passage of the years the Princess's behaviour had become more and more eccentric as she displayed almost nymphomaniac tendencies. Lady Bessborough, on a foreign tour, had been shocked by an extraordinary apparition at a ball.

> In the room was a short, very fat elderly woman, with an extremely red face (owing I suppose to the heat) in a girl's white frock-looking dress, with the shoulders, back and neck quite low (disgustingly so) down to the middle of her stomach; very black hair and eyebrows, which gave her a fierce look, and a wreath of light pink roses on her head . . . Suddenly she nodded and smiled at me, and not recollecting her I was convinced she was mad, till William Bentinck pushed me and said, 'Do you not see the Princess of Wales nodding at you?'

Having compromised her reputation by her flirtations, if no worse, with men in public life in England, she had in later years turned to servants and in particular a handsome young Italian named Pergami, whom she had picked up on her travels and made her Chamberlain. Nevertheless when the new King at length persuaded his dithering ministers that he must divorce her, it appeared to most people to be a case of the pot calling the kettle black.

It was therefore a very apprehensive Government which brought in a Bill of Pains and Penalties to dissolve the marriage on the grounds, primarily, of Caroline's adultery. Such apprehensions proved highly justified. The mass of discontent which existed in the country used the case as a means of demonstrating its opposition to established authority. No one was more skilful at supplying ammunition for this campaign than Henry Brougham, once more counsel for the defence, when the matter came before the House of Lords. Nor was he above threatening to call the King's own mistress as a defence witness to redress the balance.

Seemingly damning evidence had been obtained from eye witnesses concerning Caroline's relationship with Pergami: he had been present at her toilette when her bosom was completely bare, he had been seen coming out of her room on one occasion with only his drawers on and going into it another time wearing only his shirt. During a sea voyage to the Holy Land he had been present when she was having a bath and then spent the night in her tent on deck. So shifty and unreliable did many of the witnesses prove, however, that the King's ministers despaired. Day after day as the sordid evidence was publicly aired, with the defence making as many pertinent comparisons as possible with the King's own lifestyle, the Crown sank deeper into the mire. The London mob had a field day. Even the Duke of Wellington was stopped and forced to cry 'God Save the Queen' – 'Well gentlemen,' he responded, with his usual panache, 'since you will have it so, "God Save the Queen" – and may all your wives be like her'. When, in the course of the trial, there were quoted Christ's words to the woman caught in adultery, 'Go away and sin no more', some wit invented the famous invocation:

> Most gracious Queen we thee implore
> To go away and sin no more;
> Or if that effort be too great,
> To go away at any rate.

Unfortunately Caroline did not take the hint. Instead, when the Bill was eventually voted on, the Government's majority became so small that the Cabinet, to the King's consternation, insisted the divorce must be dropped. Though a resolution was passed that Caroline should not be crowned with her husband this was exactly what she sought to do, only to find Westminster Abbey locked against her. It is said that soon afterwards, when news of Napoleon's death arrived and George IV was told his greatest enemy was dead, he replied eagerly 'Is she, by God'. Fortunately for him Caroline's early death removed this enemy also. The washing of so much royal dirty linen in public was not easily forgotten, and as George became broken down in health, as the corsets had to be left off and the paint was no longer able to disguise the effects of an ill-spent life, he became more and more of a recluse, afraid to trust himself to the reception he might receive in his capital city.

For some years, though, his love life continued to supply him with fresh diversions. The commencement of the new reign corresponded roughly with Lady Hertford's fall from favour. Once more a middle-aged matronly figure, this time Elizabeth Marchioness Conyngham, took the royal lover by storm. Lady Hertford, now, in Princess Lieven's words, 'a luxurious abundance of flesh', was disgusted. 'She finds the new love ridiculous in view of the age of the contracting parties' – which was strange as Lady Conyngham and Lady Hertford were the same age. But then the lady who had been cast off was heard to protest that 'intimately as she had known the King, she had never ventured to speak to him on the subject of his mistresses'. Like her discarded predecessors she resented her treatment and vented her anger publicly. She, too, supported Queen Caroline's cause and continued to trouble her old love whenever she could.

As for the new love of the new reign, Lady Cowper reported from Brighton that Lady Conyngham 'sails about here in great glory very proud of her situation and he says that he never was so in love before in his life, that he's quite ashamed of being so boyish'. A few months later, observing the King's obese figure crammed into a carriage with the equally ample Marchioness, Princess Lieven had to admit 'I have never seen a man more in love'. She found his passion the more surprising as the object of it was both vulgar and foolish: 'Not an idea in her head; not a word to say for herself; nothing but a hand to

111

accept pearls and diamonds with, and an enormous balcony to wear them on.' Looking round her drawing room, 'like a fairy's boudoir', the balcony's owner was frank enough to admit 'What a pity now if all this were to end'. Whether she administered to the King's sexual needs is doubtful. It would be surprising if this gross gout-ridden figure now yearned for anything more than romance accompanied by sheeps' eyes and holding hands. At least Lady Conyngham exuded greater warmth than her predecessor; and, like Lady Hertford, she had a ready-made family to offer him.

Though she had little respect for Lady Conyngham's intellect, Princess Lieven thought her 'just the kind of malicious fool who might do a great deal of harm'. She certainly had an acquisitive instinct, losing little time in acquiring a valuable collection of jewels, and from the beginning was on the look-out for jobs for her family and friends. The Tory Cabinet was immediately on its guard. Lady Hertford, whatever her faults, came from a Tory family whereas the Conynghams were tainted with Whiggism, and the Marchioness's brother was actually in opposition in Parliament. Lord Liverpool, the Prime Minister, tended to be impatient of the King's interference in any case, and where he suspected the mistress's influence at work he was inclined to dig his toes in on even small matters. Thus, for instance, he thwarted the King by insisting on his right to nominate a Canon of Windsor after Lady Conyngham had pushed her son's tutor. Later Princess Lieven witnessed the lesson the favourite had learnt from such experiences. On the day the Master of the Buckhounds died she was asked by Lady Conyngham whether she had anyone to nominate for the vacancy.

'Are you joking?'
'Not at all. Today we can give it to whom we like. I have nobody in view in whom I am interested; and if you name someone it will be done this evening; for tomorrow Lord Liverpool will have a candidate to name to the King, and it will be too late.'

Sure enough, a letter arrived from Lord Liverpool next morning.

When Lord Hertford resigned his post as Lord Chamberlain the Government prevented the King from putting the seal to his new liaison by appointing Lord Conyngham. Rebuffs such as this, which frustrated the monarch and caused resentment to the mistress, helped place almost intolerable strains on relations between George IV and his ministers. Furthermore, party alignments in the House of Commons were such as to prevent the monarch from finding a new administration as easily as had been the case in former days. Still, the ministers' efforts to retain control appeared to have gone to extreme lengths. The King's kind heart was well matched by Lady Conyngham's, but even their efforts to secure clemency for convicted prisoners were more often than not frustrated by the Home Secretary, Sir Robert Peel, as anxious as Liverpool to resist such pressures. Though the powers of the Crown had contracted considerably since the previous century, to be denied influence in even minor matters was a cause of understandable annoyance to George IV.

Any surreptitious influence the mistress might have over foreign affairs was watched for most carefully. Princess Lieven, herself a spy for her lover Metternich, told Vienna when Lady Conyngham came to the fore that, 'although we no longer live in the times when Madame de Pompadour directed the politics of Europe, I do not regard this London revolution as entirely without significance'. Lord Castlereagh, the Foreign Secretary, having formerly enjoyed the benefits of kinship to Lady Hertford, now had to bear the new favourite's resentment. The effect of such hard feelings was limited, however. To the King, Castlereagh was infinitely preferable to the most likely alternative, Canning.

If any woman could bring influence to bear on George IV in foreign affairs, it was Princess Lieven herself. She was a young, attractive, mentally stimulating woman with whom George tried on one occasion to have an affair. ('Heaven made us for one another' was his unsuccessful ploy.) On Metternich's behalf the Ambassadress set out to persuade the King to attend the Congress of the more reactionary European powers at Verona, and as he would not go without Lady Conyngham she worked on her too. In the end the King decided to stay at home largely, the Ambassador's wife thought, because Lord Liverpool had frightened him. Bitterly she complained 'I have to deal with two women – the King and his mistress'. She came to the conclusion that 'the last person to speak to him carries the day', but as time went on she became convinced (and with justification) that the influence of Sir William Knighton, the Royal Physician and Keeper of the Privy Purse, far exceeded that of the mistress – 'He is head over heels in love, yet his doctor's influence rules him in the first place'.

It was Castlereagh's suicide that brought about the first great ministerial crisis of the reign. Liverpool pressed for Canning to succeed him and the King resisted the suggestion. Had not Canning, after his previously suspect relationship with Caroline, refused to take any part in the activity against her when she returned to England, thus confirming the old suspicion of 'extreme intimacy' in the King's mind? His promotion at home apparently blocked, Canning had decided to accept the post of Govenor-General of India when Castlereagh died. Though Liverpool's pressure eventually succeeded in achieving his appointment as Foreign Secretary, the King gave way in such a manner as to make Canning say it was like being given a ticket to Almack's inscribed 'Admit the Rogue'.

In the five years he was Foreign Secretary Canning used his position to build up his standing at court. He knew not only that he had the King's suspicion to overcome but that there was a powerful inner clique working against him. As the King's life increasingly centred round the *Cottage Orné* he had built for himself in the depths of Windsor Great Park, there gathered round him the 'Cottage Coterie' which included Lady Conyngham, Princess Lieven and a number of European diplomats. For a long time this group worked on George IV to get rid of Canning, who was rightly regarded as being less sympathetic than Castlereagh to reactionary regimes. Even if he had wanted to the King was not in a position to get rid of his Foreign Secretary. In any case, with the passage of time he came to appreciate Canning's usefulness. When a suitable opportunity occurred to help the King, the minister used it to advantage, so that, for example, when Lord Ponsonby, with whom Lady Conyngham had once been in love, suddenly returned to England, Canning responded to a royal supplication by quickly arranging for the former lover to be despatched to a post in Buenos Aires.

Canning saw that another useful route to royal favour was through the mistress herself. Not bothering to emulate Lord

Liverpool's jealous attitude towards patronage, he did his utmost to ingratiate himself with Lady Conyngham by throwing what appointments he could her way. He even made her son his own Under-Secretary. 'I should have been a fool not to take advantage of it,' laughed Lady Conyngham. 'It was the cleverest move he could make,' echoed the King. As a result of such assistance in small matters, without in any way altering his basic policies, Canning achieved his objectives. In 1826 Princess Lieven, after visiting the Cottage, reported 'We had Mr Canning there as an intimate for the first time'. When, a year later, Lord Liverpool's collapse and resignation forced the King to look for a new Prime Minister it was his co-operative Foreign Secretary, and Lady Conyngham's friend, that he selected. Unfortunately for Canning his success was short lived. In a few months he was dead.

In the last years of the reign it was the Duke of Wellington who was Prime Minister. Shortly after his appointment Canning's more liberal friends resigned, but the Duke was relieved to note 'all the women are with us'. Later when his basically anti-Catholic ministry felt obliged to promote the emancipation of the Catholics, Wellington also had occasion to be grateful that in this matter the mistress, unlike the monarch, was his ally. She had already been described as 'a protectress of the Catholics' by Princess Lieven, who had earlier found her surrounded by books of theology combatting her royal lover's view that his Coronation Oath enjoined him to preserve the *status quo*. Her views on the subject remained unchanged, and during the period when King and country were racked by the subject Wellington found her and Knighton powerful allies. 'Every man about the King favours emancipation', lamented one of his reactionary brothers. 'And every women too' echoed another. Protestant extremists came to hate Lady Conyngham so much that the Prime Minister warned his Sovereign not to receive a petition from some of them 'or opportunity will be taken to attack Lady C'.

Lady C's views on emancipation carried the day but by this time the joy she had originally given her royal lover had long since evaporated. Almost from the outset their relationship had blown hot and cold. In 1820 Princess Lieven considered there was 'nothing worse about this affair than its absurdity . . . an amorous and inconstant sexagenarian who, at

115

the beginning of his reign, gives up all his time to a love affair'. Two years later she was reporting 'the favourite does nothing but yawn'. 'The King is bored to death; he sees nobody; the favourite does not go near him. She is having an attack of prudishness.' Next month George's ardour was as keen as ever. 'If she were a widow, as I am a widower,' he was heard to declare, 'it would not be for long.' Then the following year the Ambassadress looked round during a particularly dreary evening at the Cottage: 'The King was gazing at Lady Conyngham with an expression in which somnolence battled against love; Lady Conyngham was gazing at a beautiful emerald on her arm.' As the King well knew, the jewellery and the patronage were necessary to keep her attached to him in his secluded and constricted way of life. 'She does not love him, and shows her distaste for him; and he sees it, but although he feels she is a fool, and has told me so a score of times he feels he is too old to contract fresh habits and a habit he must have.'

As he advanced in his sixties, and came to rely on drugs, the cruel caricatures of his huge bulk, often shown with the ample Lady Conyngham, did nothing to encourage him to break his seclusion. More than ever in his life he needed a woman to turn to and, with Lady Conyngham in attendance, he continued his habit of turning to her. 'With my age and infirmity,' he told the Duke of Wellington, 'it is not worthwhile looking for another.' The lady could be gracious when it suited her, and the young Princess Victoria, herald of a new age, was to retain a life-long recollection of her kindness. More often she chose to be disagreeable, interested only in the rich pickings.

She was still in attendance in the middle of 1830 when he was sixty-seven and it was obvious his end was near. It was at this stage that Mrs Fitzherbert could not refrain from breaking a self-imposed silence of twenty years. 'My anxiety respecting your Majesty,' she wrote to the man she still cared so much about, 'has got the better of my scruples.' It became clear now that his old affection for her had also remained, as he eagerly read her letter and retained it under his pillow. The Duke of Wellington observed that he wore her miniature round his neck till he died. And it was in accordance with his precise instructions that interred with him was *the picture of my beloved wife, my Maria Fitzherbert* . . . suspended round my neck by a ribbon as I used to wear it when I lived, *and placed right upon my heart*'.

When this news, confirming that in spite of all his follies and infidelities he had never ceased loving her, was conveyed to Mrs Fitzherbert it was observed that 'some large tears fell from her eyes'.

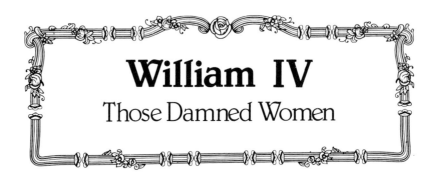

William IV
Those Damned Women

The prince who was to become William IV on George IV's death shared with his predecessor the misfortune of having George III as his well-meaning but disastrous father. In some ways William suffered a worse fate than his brothers. For from his sheltered palace childhood he was thrust, at the age of thirteen, into the barbarity and privations of the eighteenth-century Royal Navy. The results hoped for by his parents – a gainful occupation which would produce a well-disciplined young man able to avoid the pitfalls and fleshpots of this world – never accrued. To anyone less blinkered than George III it would have been obvious that a naval career starting at the rank of midshipman was hardly likely, in that era, to turn an inexperienced boy into a cultivated prince, still less an innocent child into an adult paragon of moral rectitude. It was not long before the harassed parent discovered his mistake.

Young William was soon on active service in the American War of Independence. (While his ship was wintering at New York there were even plans laid with General Washington's approval to take him prisoner, though they were never put into effect.) It was during these years that the young Prince, naturally of an open and easy-going nature, absorbed a naval bluffness that was to be his hallmark in life. His natural exuberance and affability became combined with a certain boorishness and a touch of buffoonery; and alongside his hail-fellow-well-met approach he acquired the manners and the language of the quarter-deck. In consequence, and unlike his friend Nelson who came from much more lowly stock, William was never quite a gentleman. In public life, monarchs and politicians were to cringe at his crudities, and in fashionable drawing-rooms genteel mammas would be sick with apprehension at the unexpected words their blushing daughters might hear fall from his royal lips.

As well as developing into almost a caricature of a jolly tar the Prince found that naval life, with all its rootlessness and uncertainty, gave ample scope for what his brother Frederick called 'his natural inclination for all kinds of dissipation'. Not only did he become accustomed to hard drinking and brawling but he acquired the sexual habits of a tom-cat. From an early age he had, like the rest of his family, a pronounced weakness for the fair sex. He easily fell in love – but what opportunity was there in his circumstances for true love to run smooth? His first recorded affair was a case in point. When he was home on leave at the age of fifteen he proved he already had an eye for beauty by falling for pretty young Julia Fortescue at a palace ball. The assignations which followed soon became known to his parents and he was quickly sent back to sea. This set a pattern from which it was to prove almost impossible to break out. Though he might yearn for respectable romance with some of the girls he met, the Royal Marriages Act forbade him to enter into matrimony without his father's consent, and it was obvious that no marriage other than to a foreign princess would be consented to. Knowing full well the strong sexual passions his sons had inherited, George III would have been well-advised to have contracted such marriages for them early in life. Instead he moralised while they played fast and loose.

These circumstances affected William in a peculiar fashion. It became his habit to pursue respectable women up to a certain point. Then he would satisfy himself with the less respectable, having frequent recourse, during breaks from active service, to women of easy virtue who were happy to gratify a royal lover, or to downright whores. During the two years of his late teens, when he was temporarily withdrawn from the navy in order to complete his education in Hanover, this pattern became clearly defined. He fell in love with a cousin when he was eighteen and she fourteen, but his family quickly put a stop to that. (There was even a rumour that he secretly married the daughter of the general responsible for his brother's military training, Caroline von Lingsingen: if he had done so, such a marriage would have been no more valid than his brother's to Mrs Fitzherbert.) His loftier notions nipped in the bud, he then turned elsewhere for gratification. Though he proclaimed 'the highest crime in Heaven next to murder is that of debauching innocent women', those already debauched, in the brothels of Hanover for instance, he thought fair game. Not that German prostitutes appear to have attracted him greatly. 'Oh for England,' he wrote to one of his brothers, 'and the pretty girls of Westminster, at least to such as would not clap or pox me every time I —ed.' His letter in the Royal Archives shows that he used the old Anglo-Saxon word in full so that there would be no mistake about his meaning.

Back in the navy, when he was nineteen he fell for Sir Henry Martin's daughter Sarah – 'we dance and amuse ourselves vastly well' – till her father sent her out of the way knowing no good could come of it. Though William went on loving 'my dearest S' for some time, it was not as a royal mistress that Sarah was to go down in history but in a more innocent fashion as author of 'Old Mother Hubbard'. When, a year or two later, the Prince came back from a long absence abroad it was a Plymouth merchant's daughter called Sally Winne who caught his fancy. This time it was his own father who heard of it and sent him back to sea. Again the young man had to look elsewhere for gratification. At one time it was the accommodating American wife of the Surveyor-General to whom he turned. At other times it was reported of him, 'He would go into any house where he saw a pretty girl, and was perfectly acquainted with every house of a certain description in the town'. It was by no means the most satisfying existence. 'Those damned women cause me more uneasiness than enough,' he told the Prince of Wales from North America. Another time at Plymouth he recorded: 'Dulness rules here altogether, but what is worse than all, not a woman fit to be touched with the tongs.'

To the Prince's father out of sight was usually out of mind, and except for occasional letters stuffed with moral precepts, George III can be blamed for long periods of total neglect of his son. When the Prince was either home on leave or had otherwise drawn attention to himself, his 'love of low company', his drinking, his fund of dirty stories, and his heartiness, so ill-becoming a Prince of the Blood, provoked outbursts of parental disapproval. A visit home, William discovered, was an invitation to 'a family lecture for immorality, vice, dissipation and expense, and ... the appellation of the prodigal son'. Such lectures had no effect. 'Fatherly admonitions at our time of life,' William told his brother at the advanced age of twenty-three, 'are very unpleasant and of no use.'

The King's low opinion of his sailor son was to have more important repercussions when it came to professional advancement. When William had a disagreement with the Admiralty over a disciplinary case in the West Indies he got no support from his father. So, with his promotion in the navy blocked, he returned to civilian life at the age of twenty-four. All he had to console him was the title of Duke of Clarence, rather reluctantly bestowed, and a limited allowance from a father who believed in keeping his sons short of cash and then wondered why they got into financial difficulties.

The new Duke established himself in a suite of rooms in St. James's Palace and seemed set on the same road to hell, paved with excessive drinking, excessive gambling, excessive debts and excessive womanising, which was being followed so enthusiastically by the Prince of Wales and which earned for the sons of George III so much public disgust. Fortunately, William turned out to have some saving graces. For one thing he always retained a straightforwardness and bluntness which meant that, even if he did not command respect, at least he was rarely disliked. His very directness was apt to reduce his hearers to speechlessness, as when he turned to a lady in an inn, after the break-up of the Prince of Wales' marriage, and opined:

> My brother has behaved very foolishly. To be sure he has married a very foolish, disagreeable person, but he should have made the best of a bad bargain, as my father has done. What do you think, Madam?

He also turned out to have a yearning to settle down to domestic pleasures. True to his old form, he had not been long ashore before he acquired a mistress of doubtful antecedents. Her name was Polly Finch, and the establishment he set up

121

with her in Richmond was much frowned on by the respectable society of that respectable town. But Miss Finch soon tired of this talkative and tiresome old salt. Her departure made way for William's most permanent relationship, a happy liaison of twenty years' duration.

It began in the year 1790 when the Duke of Clarence was twenty-five. His new love, who was a few years his senior, called herself Mrs Jordan. Actually she was a Miss Bland who, because of her illegitimate children, had felt it desirable to adopt a more appropriate title. Her first child had been to Richard Daly, the Dublin theatre manager who had seduced her, and the others to Sir Richard Ford with whom she had fallen in love but who had made no effort to marry her. When the Duke of Clarence met her she was a well-established actress. In addition to having some talent she had good looks and a good figure. The shape of her legs ensured her popularity in what are now called principal-boy roles, and her patent jollity and infectious laughter made her a great success in comedy. 'Her smile had the effect of sunshine,' wrote the admiring William Hazlitt, 'and her laugh did one good to hear'. Her 'fine animal spirits' proved a strong attraction to her new lover.

The news of the royal conquest was soon public knowledge. 'That the *Jordan* has crossed the *Ford*,' wrote *The Times*, 'is a matter no longer to be doubted, and the Royal Admiral has hoisted his flag.' Young William was delighted to tell his brother 'You may safely congratulate me on my success'. Before long the couple had set up house together. Mrs Jordan was a decent woman, having more in common with her fellow-actress Nell Gwyn than with 'Perdita' Robinson. She provided William with a happy home background to compensate for the frustration brought about by his aborted naval career. She made a good hostess whose hospitality his brothers were happy to enjoy. Even his father, tacitly acknowledging that if his son had to live in sin he could do worse than live with Mrs Jordan, was complacent enough to go to Drury Lane to see her act.

For she continued in her career – when it was not interrupted by her numerous pregnancies. If a further bond between her and the Duke of Clarence was needed, it was provided by the family life which resulted from the ten children of the liaison. William gave them the surname FitzClarence and (somewhat impertinently it might be thought) christian names such as George, Frederick, Augustus, Mary and Amelia, then in common use in the Royal Family itself. He and his lady proved exemplary parents, bringing up five boys and five girls in a happy home environment, first at St. James's and later at Bushy Park where the Duke became Ranger.

Money was their greatest worry. There was never enough of it. William continued to be treated as a bachelor prince although he owed money even before he met Mrs Jordan. Over the years more and more of his income had to be used to service his debts. Though he made her an allowance, she was always in need of more. In addition to supporting their own growing family, she had her previous children and various other impecunious relations dependent on her. All this, combined with a chronic inability to economise, left her, too, permanently in debt. Therefore, whenever she could, she continued to act, with all the hectic touring up and down the country that this involved.

After two decades of living together it was on the rock of money, not on any quarrel or incompatibility, that their relationship broke. With Mrs Jordan growing older and fatter, and presumably less attractive in boy's clothes, their combined debts continued to mount. The future appeared bleak as the needs of their children increased and the necessity of launching them properly in life became more imperative. 'Money is, as you know, my object,' William at length confessed, 'and I am now come to that time in life that I must make those sacrifices I would not formerly have done; but then I am a father of ten children and it is my duty to provide for them.' He decided that the only solution was to seek salvation through a suitable marriage. Unfortunately Mrs Jordan, poor woman, was kept quite in the dark as to his determination until a very late stage. She was on tour when he appears finally to have made up his mind, but having then re-established herself at Bushy with the ultimatum 'Here I stick', she had to submit to a great deal of haggling over financial arrangements and the care of their children. Eventually, at the end of 1811, matters were sorted out amicably: she was given a generous allowance, together with the care of their daughters on condition she did not return to the stage.

She took it philosophically. She had had many knocks in her life and now blamed the lack of money entirely for what had happened. Unfortunately for her, her own delicate financial condition soon suffered a severe crisis when she was saddled with the debts of an unscrupulous son-in-law, husband of one of her daughters by Richard Ford. Knowing William's own continuing difficulties she tried approaching his brothers, but neither the Regent nor any of the other princes offered assistance. In these circumstances she had no alternative but to return to the stage, thus losing the company and control of her daughters. Now fat and fifty, her charms disappearing fast, she soon lost her health as well. In 1815 she had to flee abroad to escape a debtors' prison. A year later, still in exile, she died in poverty and misery, and alone.

Though William retained a life-long affection for Mrs Jordan, there had been something cold and calculating in his decision to break with her. It was perhaps the cruellest act of his life. Its timing was also significant. The mind of his old father had just clouded over for the last time, and it appeared possible that, with his brother now in the saddle as Prince Regent, a rich marriage with a commoner might be allowed. Indeed, when the Duke decided to make the separation, he already had a prospective bride in mind. She was Catherine Tylney-Long, whom he described as 'bewitching' and 'a lovely nice little angel'. She also had a bewitching, lovely, nice and large income of £40,000 a year. Though the Duke of Clarence gave the appearance of being head over heels in love for the first time, it was obviously the heiress's ability to solve his financial problems which was her particular attraction. In any case Miss Tylney-Long found little to commend this middle-aged royal suitor, his Hanoverian heaviness of manner and appearance overlaid with naval heartiness. Instead she married the handsome young nephew of the Duke of Wellington, William Wellesley-Pole. Too late, as her spendthrift husband squandered her fortune, did she realise that perhaps a domesticated Duke, with all his idiosyncracies, might have been better after all.

Undeterred by this disappointment the Duke of Clarence began to look elsewhere and began a seven-year search for a bride which, at a time when the Royal Family's reputation was low enough already, helped degrade the standing of the Crown still further. William made himself more ridiculous looking for a wife than he had ever done in living with a mistress. Among his other sorties, overtures to the Dowager Lady Downshire, Miss Mercer Elphinstone and Lady Charlotte Lindsay met with most peremptory rejections. The widowed Countess of Berkeley appeared to be more willing, but this high-sounding lady had originally been one Mary Cole, a butcher's daughter who had been Lord Berkeley's mistress for many years before he deigned to marry her. The Prince Regent found her 'bourgeois vulgarity' unbearable, and though bourgeois vulgarity would probably have suited the Duke of Clarence very well, when it became obvious that the Regent drew the line at having the butcher's daughter as his sister-in-law even William had to desist. His attempt to secure the Grand Duchess of Oldenburg, sister of the Emperor of Russia, appeared more seemly. Unfortunately, when they met, the Grand Duchess, like others before her, found his uncouth manners and vulgar familiarity insufferable and would have nothing to do with him. Nor would his cousin Princess Sophia of Gloucester.

After years of fruitless effort, with Mrs Jordan already dead, William was no nearer his goal. The death of the Regent's daughter in 1817, putting the Duke of Clarence in the direct line of succession, increased the necessity for a suitable match. Even so, attempts to secure the hand of two Hessian princesses and the suggestion of the Princess Royal of Denmark came to nothing. By now 'William and his little concerns' were beginning to put the Duke's sanity in doubt and becoming the despair of his family. To its even greater despair he continued to fall most unsuitably in love. Now the object of his affections was another English heiress, the pretty, if somewhat eccentric, Miss Wyckham. Though some thought her vulgar, William called her a 'dear sweet angel' and was determined to marry her. On hearing the news the Prince Regent was heard to groan. Miss Wyckham actually accepted the proffered hand but when the Government made its opposition clear William drew back and Miss Wyckham stepped down gracefully. (He was later able to reward her with a peerage.)

The hunt became more frantic. The Government, anxious to secure the succession to the throne, was now proving more

125

co-operative, promising to raise the Duke's allowance substantially and reduce his debts if he found a suitable wife. Eventually he achieved what some were beginning to think impossible. An offer was made for the hand of Princess Adelaide of Saxe-Meiningen and gladly accepted. At twenty-six Adelaide had been practically on the shelf. The bachelor Prince was now fifty-two, old enough to be her father. Nevertheless they turned out to be remarkably suited to one another. She proved to be no beauty, 'a poor wishy-washy thing' and 'very ugly with a horrid complexion' were typical descriptions, but then her fat and balding spouse was no oil-painting either. Both were highly domesticated, he was good-natured and she tolerant and ingratiating enough to soften his manners. Above all she was happy to accept his brood of illegitimate children. The marriage was not blessed with the birth of strong babies – none survived infancy – so the bastard family provided some outlet for Adelaide's maternal instincts.

When Adelaide arrived, William's children fell into virtually two generations, ranging from George who was twenty-four to Amelia who was only eleven. Though their father's income did not increase as much as he had hoped, so limiting his ability to help them financially, as they each became of marriageable age he did his best to help them make good marriages. The bar sinister was perpetuated in two cases, when George married an illegitimate daughter of Lord Egremont and Mary the illegitimate son of William's old friend Lord Holland, but both were respectable connections. All the other daughters made good marriages, one becoming Lady Erroll, another Lady Falkland and another the future Lady De L'Isle and Dudley. When the girls married they took on the status of their husbands. The boys, in spite of good marriages, had no status at all and felt their position most severely. George took the matter so much to heart he was to quarrel constantly with his father and, still unreconciled to his lot, to commit suicide five years after the old man's death.

Serious trouble began when, as he was approaching sixty-five, William came to the throne. His accession, following as it did the earlier follies and final seclusion of his brother, took place at a time when the monarchy's prestige in Britain was at its lowest ebb. It was a time for kings to tread softly: with the almost coincidental fall of the restored Bourbons in France there was a whiff of revolution in the air. Though the new King was seen to lack dignity (he was observed to spit through his carriage window, and at a ball Washington Irving saw him wipe his nose with the back of his forefinger) nevertheless he was well-meaning, affable and had certain domestic virtues which, with the help of Queen Adelaide, restored a degree of respectability to the throne. What many found hard to reconcile with this respectability was the way in which he openly accepted the presence of his bastard children. Though some courtiers welcomed the liveliness which the high-spirited FitzClarences brought to a relatively dull existence at court, and many enjoyed seeing the King's happiness at now being surrounded by his grandchildren, criticism was not lacking. *The Morning Post* was incensed at the 'impudence and rapacity of the FitzJordans'. 'Can anything be more indecent,' it asked, 'than the entry of a Sovereign into his capital, with one bastard riding before him, and another by the side of his carriage?'

Though he was unwilling to deprive himself of the presence of his offspring the King was wise enough to realise that, in the social and political climate of the time, he needed to tread carefully when it came to advancing his children. This his sons, led by the eldest, were unwilling to accept. Soon after the accession they wrote pointing out their 'cruel position' and demanding the kind of 'reparation which your predecessors had not failed to exert'. They demanded titles to give them social position, a peerage for the eldest, a status equal at least to the sons of dukes for the others. Then they wanted places and pensions to give them financial security. As Greville put it: 'They want to renew the days of Charles II instead of waiting patiently and letting the King do what he can for them.'

They refused to realise that times had changed. The patronage of the Crown had shrunk, Government permission had to be received for most things, and there was now the formidable obstacle of public opinion for the Government to contend with. William wished to provide his sons with the financial wherewithal to support their position in life before he enhanced their status, but he knew he must progress little by little. 'Pray be *prudent* and *patient* and *do give him time,*' one of his brothers advised the bastards. This they refused to do.

127

A violent quarrel ensued and they withdrew themselves and their families from court. Frederick even threatened to stand for Parliament. Had he been elected the scandal would have further undermined his father's position at a time when it was being rendered untenable enough by the vicissitudes of the great Reform Bill.

A few months later a family peace was patched up. Backed by money from his father-in-law, Lord Egremont, to support his new position, George was made Earl of Munster. (He did not fail to point out that Charles II's natural sons had been made dukes.) The other sons were given the status of the younger sons of a marquess. Still not satisfied, the new Earl of Munster had the arrogance to plague his father with the suggestion that he carry the crown at the Coronation. 'What is more fit than your own flesh and blood?' William could think of few who were less fit. Another quarrel was followed by another reconciliation. Lord Munster was now made Constable of the Round Tower at Windsor, a post which brought with it an income, and even admitted to the Privy Council. He was still dissatisfied with his lot and his unreasonable demands continued to harass his father. 'I fear that his presence will be a source of excitement and irritation,' the King's private secretary wrote to the Prime Minister, 'indeed the effects of his last visit are still very perceptible.' Other sons also continued to be troublesome. Frederick bombarded his father with requests to be made a Hanoverian General. Augustus had taken the cloth but was singularly lacking in the Christian virtue of humility: he demanded promotion and was then apt to be insulted by what was offered him. A post at Worcester Cathedral was indignantly rejected, and even to be made a Canon of Windsor he did not think good enough.

As well as helping to make his personal life miserable, William's family troubles had their repercussions on his relationship with Lord Grey's Whig Government. When Grey was made a Knight of the Garter it was given out by disgruntled Tories that this was a sop to him for allowing William to make his eldest son a peer. But as the move for Parliamentary Reform gathered momentum the FitzClarence sons were among those known to oppose the Government's policies. Queen Adelaide was also widely suspected of prejudicing the King against his ministers, a suspicion which deepened when her Chamberlain, the Tory Lord Howe, more than once publicly demonstrated his anti-government feelings. Curiously enough it was the obvious partiality of the otherwise highly-proper Queen for her good-looking Chamberlain that provided one of the biggest subjects for gossip during the reign. The story that on the morning of his accession William had declared that he was going back to bed 'as he had long wished to sleep with a queen' is probably apocryphal. He continued to sleep in the same room as his wife (according to one of his sons, in a separate bed) but there was never any likelihood of further children. When therefore a false rumour was started that Adelaide was pregnant the old man's response was 'Damned stuff '. The wits however had a field day – 'Oh Lord Howe wonderful are thy ways!' Though the Queen's relations with her Chamberlain were almost certainly as pure as those of the future Queen Alexandra with her ardent admirer Edwin Montagu, Adelaide was exceedingly upset when the Government, after Howe's Tory outbursts, insisted on his resignation. Eventually he was restored to office on the understanding that he behaved with more political circumspection in future.

Adelaide and the FitzClarences continued to show barely concealed distaste for the kind of reforms the Government insisted on carrying through. 'All the Royal Family, bastards and all, have been incessantly at the King,' recorded Greville, the Clerk of the Privy Council. When the House of Lords rejected the Reform Bill Lord Munster, during one of his temporary reconciliations with his father, passed on to the Opposition his own interpretation of William's views. Such attempts at trouble-making proved abortive. The King, albeit most reluctantly at times, went along with his ministers so that a constitutional crisis was averted. The FitzClarences were mischievous rather than influential. Nevertheless, had it become public knowledge that they were seeking to exert influence on the Sovereign against the Government at such a critical time there might have been serious political repercussions. Even Adelaide found them unreliable as allies. When the King later called in Peel to form a Tory administration (which proved to be short-lived), and the Queen's influence was suspected, the bastards were in the van of those who criticised the poor woman.

Though the King's daughters and their husbands could sometimes be difficult, he had an easier relationship with them than with his sons. He was never happier than when surrounded by his children and a brood of boisterous grandchildren. Except for an aptitude for prolix speechifying, and a tendency to fall back on naval epithets when he lost his temper, he was now the epitome of domesticity. Yet his legitimate heir, his niece Victoria, was conspicuous by her absence from his court. This was no fault of hers. She was a sweet unaffected child, eleven years old when her Uncle William came to the throne, and always regarded him with affection. When Adelaide had lost her babies she had said to Victoria's mother, the Duchess of Kent, 'My children are dead, but your child lives, and she is mine too'. This was not to be.

The Duchess of Kent distrusted most of the Royal Family and was determined to keep her child apart, completely under her own domination. Later this was part of a scheme to retain mastery over the growing girl, so that in the event of her becoming Queen her mother would remain fully in control. She even contrived the tearful child's absence from William's Coronation. Such behaviour provoked the old man's wrath, the more so as it was combined with trips up and down the country designed to provide the maximum publicity for the young Princess. In her endeavours to remain aloof from the court the Duchess found the illegitimacy of the King's children a useful card to play. She objected to meeting George FitzClarence even by accident at Windsor Castle and used the effect which the presence of bastards would have on her daughter's morals as an excuse to keep Victoria away. Yet when she and her child met her own brother Leopold's mistress at Claremont, again by accident, motherly embarrassment and protectiveness did not prevent her from taking the Princess there again. In spite of her double standards, the Duchess insisted on maintaining her haughty attitude towards the King's children right to the end, so that when his daughter Lady De L'Isle died in Kensington Palace, where she was Housekeeper and where the Kents lived, Victoria's mother went ahead with a dinner party there the same evening.

The tension produced by this kind of behaviour brought about the famous scene at Windsor Castle during one of the

Duchess of Kent's rare visits when she was publicly insulted by the King in one of his bluff, rambling after-dinner speeches. As far as the future Queen Victoria was concerned, she grew up with little experience of court life, her adolescence marred by a running battle between her mother and her uncle. Luckily her uncle managed to live just long enough to enable her to reach her eighteenth birthday when she could reign alone.

Once in control, the new Queen proved more broadminded and tolerant than her mother. She allowed the FitzClarences to stay at Windsor for as long as they chose after the funeral – 'poor people, they must be very unhappy'. She did not immediately reappoint Munster as Constable. 'She imagines,' Lord Holland confided, 'he might be an unpleasant inmate' – and she was undoubtedly right. When she offered the post to her uncle, the Duke of Sussex, he suggested Munster be allowed to keep it, and in the end she agreed. But, without seeking to be unkind, the whole FitzClarence connection formed part of that chapter in the history of the Royal Family which she once described as 'ghosts best forgotten'. They gave way to more seemly visitors to court.

The Victorian era had arrived.

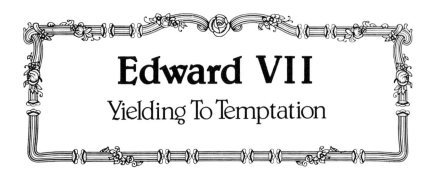

Edward VII
Yielding To Temptation

Only four years after William IV was laid to rest a new heir to the throne arrived. As Albert Edward, Prince of Wales, grew up his parents knew only too well that the world was becoming a very different place from the one in which Queen Victoria's wicked uncles had run wild. It was one of the great preoccupations of Victoria and Albert, themselves both moral and monogamous, to bring up their eldest son as a worthy heir. Knowing that further blatant immorality in the Royal Family might fatally affect the throne, they set out to produce a paragon of virtues. Yet with all their good intentions they made precisely the same mistakes – excessive regimentation and a doomed endeavour to provide insulation from the outside world – that had already bedevilled their predecessors, George III and Queen Charlotte.

To make matters worse it soon became clear that the material the young parents had to work on was itself most unpromising. Though he had an affectionate nature, Bertie, as he was known in the family, was slower and less intelligent than his elder sister with whom he was unfavourably compared. Worse still, he appeared lazy, easily bored and uninterested in serious matters. From his early youth he gave indications of being keener in the pleasures of this world than of the next. The royal couple intensified their efforts. They put the boy under tutors with a stiffer curriculum, every hour of the day being accounted for, in an attempt to isolate him and educate him into being a better man. The effect was merely to confirm him in his inclinations. The confinement and discipline of these years made him intolerant of confinement and discipline for the rest of his life, the boredom made him restlessly anxious never to be bored. He developed into the most gregarious of princes, ever anxious for gaiety and excitement.

As Albert Edward grew too old for the schoolroom his anxious parents debated how best to introduce him into the world without immediately submerging him in its pleasures. A trip to Germany when he was barely sixteen gave an early insight into the attraction of the fair sex: he became a little intoxicated one evening and kissed a pretty girl. (He was nearly seventeen, though, when, because of his obvious ignorance, the facts of life had to be explained to him – not by his parents.) His first taste in any measure of the social whirl was during his visit to Canada and the United States when he was eighteen. Then it was noted how much he preferred to dance, not with the wives of elderly worthies, but with their pretty daughters.

One thing soon became apparent to Victoria and Albert: an early marriage for their son was imperative. In his case matrimony would be literally, in the words of the marriage service, 'for a remedy against sin, and to avoid fornication'. The Prince himself could not but agree with his father's tactful suggestion that 'it would be impossible for you to lead, with any chance of success or comfort to yourself, a protracted bachelor life'. Not anxious to repeat the kind of disastrous mistake made by his great-uncle, the Regent, Albert Edward added certain conditions with regard to his bride: he would only marry someone he cared for and someone who matched up to his own exacting standards of beauty. The Queen in addition saw the importance of the young lady not only being simple and unaffected but having sufficient strength of character to keep the young Prince on the straight and narrow.

Where was such a pearl to be found? For 150 years the Protestant princesses of Germany had been the only source of brides for British princes. Now the Almanach de Gotha was searched in vain. It was only the paramount importance of finding someone their son would like that persuaded the royal parents to consider the beautiful and by all accounts fascinating Danish princess, Alexandra. She was only sixteen, three years younger than her intended bridegroom, when her good looks forced themselves on his parents' attention. Against her attractions had to be balanced the political embarrassment of her family connections, especially in view of the troubles between Denmark and Prussia that loomed on the horizon, troubles which were soon to lead to war (a war which led to a lifelong distaste for Prussia on the part of Albert Edward and his wife).

After the young prince had expressed an initial interest in Alexandra a carefully contrived accidental meeting was arranged in the Cathedral at Speyer in September 1861. This went very well. He was impressed by what he saw and his interest appeared to be reciprocated. He seemed by now though, to his parents' surprise, to be less keen on the whole idea of marriage. The reason for this change of heart was soon to become painfully obvious.

A few months previously, in the middle of a carefully shielded spell at Cambridge University, he had at last been granted his wish to spend some time with the army. With some trepidation his parents allowed him to go to The Curragh Camp for a period of training. The trepidation was brought about by the knowledge that the morals of fashionable young army officers were not the feature for which they were most noted. Sure enough, while the young prince made disappointing progress in military affairs, he made great strides in another direction. It was not long before the young bloods had spirited into his bed one Nellie Clifden, a young actress familiar to many of them. His association with her became a nightly occurrence and continued after his return to England a few weeks later. So, at the age of nineteen, in spite of so much parental care, he had lost his innocence before meeting his intended bride. It was the beginning of a lifetime of philandering that was to lead *The Times*, on his accession forty years later, to lament the fact that Albert Edward must often have prayed 'Lead us not into temptation' with what it called 'a feeling akin to hopelessness'.

While at the time of the Speyer meeting Victoria and Albert had been ignorant of their son's initiation at The Curragh, the London clubs were soon buzzing with the story. Nellie was too proud of her conquest to keep her mouth shut. When Albert eventually heard the story the young prince was already back at Cambridge. With heavy heart, feeling far from well, and declaring that in all his life nothing had given more pain, the prematurely-aged father travelled down to see his son and have the matter out. All kinds of worries, for example that Nellie might bring the Crown once more into the gutter by instituting a paternity case, raced through his mind. Bertie confessed all. After an initial resistance he had, he admitted, yielded to temptation.

With a heart scarcely lighter Prince Albert returned home. Within three weeks he was dead. Though his Cambridge trip had not helped his tired frame, worn down by overwork and worry, the typhoid germs which killed him were already incubating within him before the commencement of that sad journey. Nevertheless his grief-stricken widow could not put out of her mind the juxtaposition of events at The Curragh and her husband's premature death. Whereas her eldest son might otherwise have been her mainstay in life she now could hardly bear to look at him. Though her attitude mellowed over the years and she came to appreciate his many good qualities, by that time they had gone too far down their separate paths for her to share her work with him.

Bowed down though she was by grief, the Queen did not forget the marriage plans which now became the 'sacred duty our darling left us to perform'. She felt it wise to let Alexandra's parents know what they in fact knew already, that the intended bridegroom had lost his innocence. She was, she assured them, confident he had fully repented and 'he would make a steady husband'. Certainly he was now willing to co-operate. Alexandra's good looks and unaffected nature had grown on him, and he readily proposed to her in the garden of the Belgian King's palace at Laeken. She was equally happy to accept. After all, in addition to what he had to offer materially and socially, he was kind and affable and had a lovable quality about him. At this stage, too, he was still slim, if tending to plumpness, and not bad-looking, if somewhat chinless – he grew his beard later. Irrespective of his position, Alexandra was at pains to insist that were he a cowboy she would have loved him just the same. It was a love that enabled her to survive the trials of forty-seven years of marriage. For though the Prince of Wales, at the age of twenty-one, reached what his mother hoped would be the safe haven of matrimony, for him matrimony turned out to be not so much a safe haven as a port of call.

Everything started well. Not only did the marriage give the young couple independence and a home of their own, but it enabled them, bolstered by wealth and position, to go out and enjoy themselves, something which Alexandra appeared to take to just as much as the Prince. Deprived by his mother of any work of real importance, and with no intellectual interests to fall back on, it was hardly surprising that he was swallowed up in the social whirl. Life became a constant round of pleasure; the Queen feared that the Princess would waste away to a skeleton. Indeed, Alexandra went on with her activities till within a few hours of the birth of her first child, a boy born prematurely after eight months of marriage. Other children followed quickly. Six were born in the first eight years of marriage. The seventh died almost immediately after birth. Then the Princess, though only twenty-seven, had no more. Did this mean that the young couple ceased having marital relations? At a time when contraception was not usually practised within marriage the assumption must be that it did.

In many ways the marriage remained a considerable success. The Prince, whatever his sexual proclivities, was in his mother's words 'very domestic' and highly appreciative of the happy home background his wife was so good at providing. They were most happy at Sandringham, the Norfolk country estate that had been bought for the Prince, curiously enough after its previous owner, having married his mistress, had found it more convenient to live abroad. Both Prince and Princess were doting if not altogether successful parents and their family life provided a bond which kept the marriage together through a number of unpleasant episodes and a love-life for which the Prince of Wales became notorious. In spite of her great, and continuing, beauty and her undoubted social qualities, Alexandra in other ways did not match up to her husband's needs. She was both headstrong and scatter-brained, and she did not possess the intelligence he liked women to have in addition to physical charms. There was a permanent childishness about her, to which was added the strain of increasing deafness after she had rheumatic fever at the age of twenty-two. Still, she showed remarkable loyalty, tact and forebearance for, as Queen Victoria knew, she was

George IV – his emotions raised to ecstatic heights.

Right No longer able to disguise the effects of a mis-spent life.

Queen Caroline of Brunswick – a case of the pot calling the kettle black?

Below Caroline as the cartoonists saw her.

Mrs Fitzherbert – 'Dearer to me than life'.

'Wife or No Wife'. Gillray's cartoon portrays the secret marriage taking place between the Prince and Mrs Fitzherbert. Fox gives the bride away, Burke performs the ceremony while Lord North sleeps.

Above 'A King-fisher' – Lady Conyngham and George IV. *Below left* Lady Jersey, *below right* Lady Hertford.

ROYAL NAVY.

'Royal Navy'. William IV turns his back on his naval career to follow the signpost to domesticity with Mrs Jordan at Bushy Park.

Dorothea Jordan – shapely legs and an infectious laugh.

Queen Alexandra – 'normally tolerant'.   'Edward the Caresser'.

Lillie Langry captured the imagination of artists including, below, Millais.

Lady Warwick, 'My own adored little Daisy wife'.

Alice Keppel, the balm that was essential to keep the King going.

'Their relationship became the one thing in life that mattered to him' -- a photograph of Mrs Simpson published in the French magazine *L'Illustration* while the British papers still ignored her existence.

Thelma Lady Furness helped fill his private hours.

not blind to his extra-marital adventures. For his part, the Prince always treated her with respect, at least in public, put up readily with her imperfections, including her notorious unpunctuality, gave in to many of her whims – and in the end always came home to her.

Infidelity, if such a mild word can be used to describe the Prince's behaviour, appears to have begun early in the marriage. All his life he found beautiful women irresistible, and his wife's almost continual pregnancies of the early years must have put an intolerable strain on a man so incapable of sexual continence. Walter Bagehot, writing his *English Constitution* at this very time, drew attention to the fact that Princes of Wales over the ages had been offered 'whatever is most attractive, whatever is most seductive', and suggested: 'It is not rational to expect the best virtue where temptation is applied in the most trying form at the frailest time of human life.' This Prince of Wales was only too ready to succumb to temptation, and opportunities were freely available for him to do so. Like a butterfly he fluttered eagerly from one opportunity to another, from the most aristocratic of married women willing to have a discreet affair, to so-called actresses who were little better than common prostitutes.

He found other opportunities abroad. During his wife's second pregnancy he excused himself from the tameness of her family home in Copenhagen and popped over to Stockholm where King Charles XV of Sweden thoughtfully arranged for him to meet accommodating ladies. When the next pregnancy stopped the Princess from joining her husband in St. Petersburg for her sister's marriage, his attentions to the ladies there were soon being talked about back home. Above all at this time he developed a lifetime's habit of making trips *en garçon* to European centres of disrepute, but most of all to Paris, the sin-city of Europe both under the Second Empire and the Third Republic.

'Supper after the opera with some of the female Paris notorieties,' recorded one of his world-weary Household as typical of a trip to Paris with the Prince of Wales early in 1867. At this time the name of Hortense Schneider, famed for her performances in Offenbach operettas, was most closely linked with his. Her relations with royalty generally were to earn her the title of *'le passage des princes'*. His association with her, when it became known in England, gave further ammunition to his critics who accused him of neglecting his wife during her attack of rheumatic fever. (Even when he was in London it was noted how on one occasion, when Alexandra was seriously ill, he returned home apparently unconcerned at 3 a.m.) At other times, when staying at the Hotel Brighton as Baron Renfrew, he savoured Parisian women of lower repute, among them Giulia Barucci (by her own confession 'the greatest whore in the world') whose brother tried later (and unsuccessfully) to blackmail him. Equally, when staying at the châteaux of the French aristocracy he experienced no difficulty in finding co-operative hostesses. During a visit to Paris in 1872 he established liaisons with several leading members of the aristocracy whose husbands were prepared to turn a blind eye to the fact that their wives were having a discreet affair, while they themselves carried on rather less discreetly. The Princesse de Sagan was a particular favourite: her young son, on one occasion coming across the Prince's temporarily discarded clothes in his mother's rooms, is said to have thrown them into the fountain. Visits to Paris two or three times a year became a regular feature of the Prince's diary, and he was speaking no less than the truth when, many years later as King, in preparing the way for the *Entente Cordiale*, he uttered his famous description of Paris as the beautiful city *'où je me trouve toujours comme si j'étais chez moi'*.

In England Albert Edward built up for himself a regular way of life accommodating as many affairs of varying character as his tastes and needs required. The young Earl of Rosebery was shocked when it was put to him that he allow his London house to be used for the Prince to entertain 'actresses'. Rosebery declined, but Lord Carrington was more cooperative, and many were the chorus girls and other willing young women whom the Prince was able to meet at his home. Later there was to be a suite regularly reserved for royal 'entertaining' at Rosa Lewis's famous Cavendish Hotel in Jermyn Street.

As well as the close contacts he established with the *demi-monde*, the Prince of Wales established liaisons with outwardly respectable ladies in British society. He was able to attract them even though his looks were poor, his girth increasing and he was already going thin on top, for he was kind and well-mannered and, above all, he was socially powerful, the opener of all doors. Such affairs, in these years at any rate, were casual and usually closely guarded secrets. In this field Albert Edward did not establish new patterns so much as adopt existing ones. Though Queen Victoria, with some justification, might declare 'the country could never bear to have another George IV as Prince of Wales' the morals of the Regency had not died with George IV. Lord Melbourne, Victoria's own adored first Prime Minister, had himself been cited in two divorce actions shortly before the Queen's accession. Her first Lord Chamberlain, Lord Conyngham, son of George IV's mistress, introduced his own mistress into Buckingham Palace as Housekeeper, and Lord Palmerston, whose later career spanned the first half of her reign, had begun his close relationship with his wife many years before she was free to marry him. In exactly the same way Lord Hartington, whose political career covered the second half of the Queen's reign, had a well-known association with the Duchess of Manchester long before they were able to marry.

It was the *modus vivendi* of a previous age, perpetuated by what Queen Victoria scathingly called 'the fashionables' in society, into which the Prince of Wales threw himself enthusiastically. In the more moral climate of the Victorian Age the game had to be played with greater discretion than heretofore. The cardinal sin was to be found out. Otherwise the participants' attitude was summed up in Mrs Patrick Campbell's motto 'It doesn't matter what you do in the bedroom, as long as you don't do it in the street and frighten the horses'. The Prince of Wales became an expert in the nuances of this kind of behaviour. He developed to a fine art the custom of visiting ladies in their drawing-rooms during the afternoon. Then it was understood that the husband would be absent about his business (perhaps visiting another lady) and that no other caller would be admitted. Often a plain cab, not the Prince's own carriage with its distinctive coat of arms, would wait discreetly round the corner. (It was this kind of day-time drawing-room escapade, in an era when modes of dress were particularly complicated, which was to provoke Mrs Patrick Campbell, on her remarriage, into another famous exclamation: 'Ah, the deep, deep bliss of the double bed, after the hurly-burly of the chaise longue.') In the course of time there were certain embellishments to the game. There developed, for example, the practice of holding Saturday-to-Monday country-house parties with the peculiarly British habit of giving husband and wife separate bedrooms, something which facilitated a great deal of illicit late-night visiting.

All this had little to do with conventional middle-class morality which, except for outward forms, did not affect certain upper sections (or certain lower ones) of Victorian society too deeply. As regards preserving the outward forms Albert Edward on the whole managed very well. He is not known to have made the same mistake as one of his friends who, seeking his assignation, went into the wrong room one dark night, jumped into the bed crying 'Cock-a-doodle-do' and, when the light was lit, discovered himself between the Bishop of Chester and his wife. It was usually the Prince's friends who let him down, as when, in 1870, a demented Lady Mordaunt, having given birth to an almost-blind child, confessed adultery to her husband. He then brought a divorce action against her citing several men, including the Prince of Wales, whose names the poor woman had blurted out. All along the Prince denied the allegation, and the letters which he had written to her turned out to be harmless if indiscreet. Nevertheless the case came in for a blaze of publicity in open court, and the Prince had to give evidence to clear his name. When asked 'Has there ever been any improper familiarity or criminal act between yourself and Lady Mordaunt?' he answered with apparent conviction, 'There has not'.

The divorce action failed because the court decided that the lady was insane and unfit to plead. Unfortunately the public revelation of the Prince's mode of life and his habit, for example, of visiting ladies alone, could not but cause scandal. To make matters worse, this happened at a time when the popularity of the Crown was at a dangerously low ebb. For this the Queen was to blame even more than her son, largely because she had refused since Albert's death to show herself in public. As Gladstone put it: 'The Queen is invisible and the Prince of Wales not respected.' Ironically it was to be the Prince's recovery from the deadly typhoid fever, shortly after the Mordaunt case, that rekindled the nation's loyalty to the throne and put paid to the republican mood in the country. As far as his mother was concerned, however, the divorce scandal had merely confirmed her earlier view of his unreliability and she, in consequence, refused to agree to Gladstone's proposals aimed at putting an end to what Bagehot described as 'the most hopeless idleness' of the nation's most eminent 'unemployed youth'. Once more the pleasure-loving Prince had too much time on his hands.

Though he managed to keep secret the fact that the widowed Lady Susan Vane Tempest had a child by him, not surprisingly there were new scandals to come. One, in 1876, looked like shaking the throne to its very foundations. While accompanying the Prince of Wales on a tour of India, Lord Aylesford received a letter from his wife informing him of her intention to run away with her lover Lord Blandford. Aylesford hurried home in advance of the royal party and prepared to start divorce proceedings. At this stage Blandford's friends, led by his younger brother Lord Randolph Churchill, tried to stop the matter from becoming public. The wronged husband refused to stop the divorce action. As the Prince of Wales, by this time on his way home, refused to put pressure on Aylesford it appeared to some, including Lord Randolph, that the Prince was taking Aylesford's side. In consequence Lord Randolph decided to take more extreme action to secure his ends. He called upon the Princess of Wales and told her of his intention to publish 'most compromising' letters written by the Prince to Lady Aylesford a few years before and containing 'improper proposals'. These letters, if published, he suggested, would ensure that Alexandra's husband would 'never sit upon the throne of England'.

The Prince sent messages to his wife assuring her of his innocence; the Princess proved her loyalty to him by going down to Portsmouth to meet him on his arrival, and the same evening accompanied him to the opera. Meanwhile Albert Edward was beside himself with rage at Churchill's behaviour. His involvement of the Princess of Wales led the Prince in due course to issue him with a challenge to a duel. Though Lord Randolph airily dismissed this as impossible, the man who shortly before had claimed 'I have the Crown of England in my pocket' now found himself in very deep water indeed. The Queen loyally supported her son, and it needed all the devious diplomacy of the worldly Disraeli to sort the matter out – luckily he, and not Gladstone, was Prime Minister at the time.

Lord Aylesford agreed to drop his action, quietly arranging a separation from his wife who went to live with Blandford in Paris. As part of the arrangement Lord Randolph made an apology to the Prince, but he did it so grudgingly that he and his young American wife Jennie were virtually excluded from London's society; once the Prince of Wales let it be known he would accept hospitality from no one who entertained them, their social excommunication was assured.

At an expense he could ill afford Churchill's father, the Duke of Marlborough, agreed to Disraeli's suggestion that he remove himself from London, with Lord Randolph and his family, to become Viceroy of Ireland. Thus it was that the Churchills' infant son, Winston, was to have as his earliest recollection the years he spent in Dublin between the time he was two and five years old. On the family's return home, Lord Randolph swiftly built up for himself a reputation as one of the rising stars of the Conservative Party, and it was only at this stage, in 1883, that the Prince of Wales condescended to dine at the same table as the Churchills once again. Amicable relations were now re-established and the beautiful Jennie became one more object of the Prince's attentions.

Not that in the intervening years there had been any shortage of female diversions. As he advanced into middle age the increasingly portly Prince continued undaunted on the path of his amatory pursuits. He was excited by such varying charms as those of Sarah Bernhardt (who once informed a friend in the early hours of the morning 'I am just back from the Prince of Wales at twenty past one') and those of the American Miss Chamberlayne (mockingly referred to by Alexandra as 'Miss Chamberpots'). 'How strange,' the Duke of Cambridge was to muse at one stage, 'this new line of the Prince of Wales's, taking to young girls and discarding the married women.' It was however to be his affair with a married woman, though a young one, which formed the highlight of his middle years. Her name was Lillie Langtry.

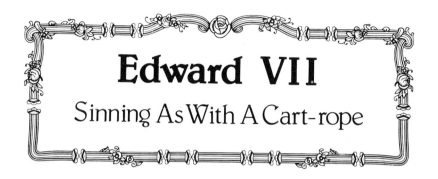

Edward VII
Sinning As With A Cart-rope

Lillie Langtry, her colourless husband reluctantly in tow, had arrived on the London scene when in her early twenties. She was of respectable but modest origins – daughter of Dean Le Breton of Jersey – and had little to recommend her to society except her beautiful face, fine figure and remarkable poise. At that time her type of beauty, rounded features with a lovely complexion, was much admired and captured the imagination of artists. Millais' picture of her holding a lily attracted widespread public admiration. Her face was literally her fortune. Though she started her social career with a single black gown, one invitation led to another and soon she was the rage of London society.

It was not long before Mrs Langtry met the Prince of Wales. Their first encounter was in 1877, and almost at once a close relationship developed between them. As well as being beautiful she was shrewd and discreet, and she managed for some years to conduct herself and her affairs in a manner acceptable to the respectable society of the period. The Princess of Wales treated her with consideration, even visiting her when she was ill, and Gladstone, who always had an eye for beauty, was among her many admirers. Unfortunately, in the course of a few years her husband became submerged in drink and debt, and as her marriage broke up her aura of respectability also began to disintegrate. At this stage she had to withdraw temporarily from the London scene to give birth to a daughter. The father is believed to have been, not the dissipated

143

Prince of Wales, but handsome, dashing Prince Louis of Battenberg, who was later, in wedlock, to father Earl Mountbatten of Burma. Even so Lillie's daughter, whose existence was long kept a close secret, was an object of Albert Edward's kindness as indeed Mrs Langtry herself continued to be.

At a time when much of London society was closing its ranks against her the Prince of Wales, with the kindness he often showed to lady friends even when the bloom had gone off their relationship, loyally supported her endeavours to make an independent living for herself by going on the stage. He cajoled his friends into joining him at her London début and helped launch her on a successful career. With business acumen rather than acting talent, her friendship with the Prince of Wales going before her to draw the crowds, she ended up a rich woman. At the same time she retained the Prince's regard. Though a London publication might proclaim 'There is nothing whatever between the Prince of Wales and Lillie Langtry' and the following week add 'Not even a sheet', she preserved her old discretion. Perhaps her greatest lapse from grace, in the eyes of the period, was to appear in an advertisement for Pears' Soap. For as long as she lived she never enlightened the world with regard to her royal love affair.

In the light of the lowly Jersey Lily's prudent behaviour, it was ironical that the woman who succeeded her in the Prince's affections, though out of a much higher social drawer, proved to be a far more talkative, flamboyant, and therefore dangerous, creature. Daisy Brooke had been a rich and beautiful heiress still in her teens when Queen Victoria had considered her as a possible wife for her youngest son, Prince Leopold. But Daisy had already fallen in love with Lord Brooke, the Earl of Warwick's heir, so the Queen dropped her son's suit. Later Victoria gave thanks for Leopold's escape from a woman who turned into a social butterfly and a fast rider to hounds – fast in more than one way as the Queen well knew.

Before the Prince of Wales came on to the scene Lord Charles Beresford, a rising star in the Royal Navy, had had an affair with her. Indeed it was the mess into which Daisy had got herself over Beresford that brought the Beauty and the Prince together. Lord Charles, to her intense annoyance, had so far re-established relations with his own wife as to make her pregnant. The jealous mistress thereupon penned a most furious demand to her erstwhile lover calling on him to reject his wife and return to her. The wife intercepted this letter and held on to it for future use. Daisy thereupon appealed to the well-known chivalry of the Prince of Wales, confiding to him her side of the story and begging his help in retrieving the letter.

The Prince of Wales, who was now approaching fifty, had already come to admire Lady Brooke and during her appeal 'I saw him looking at me in a way all women understand'. With her slim figure and fine features, and in spite of pinched lips and determined chin, she was a highly attractive woman. Though scheming and quick-witted she had the ability, most appealing to a man, to suggest helplessness. The Prince agreed to help her. The result was to bring him once again within a hair's breadth of being involved in a public washing of high society's dirty linen. First of all Lady Charles refused to give up the letter. In his anger the Prince used the strongest weapon at his disposal: he excluded her from his, and thereby from nearly all fashionable society. Her fiery husband then took up the cudgels. He had not, he declared, 'any intention of allowing any woman to wreak her vengeance on my wife because I would not accede to her entreaties to return a friendship I had repudiated'. He threatened to expose the whole business, including the part the Prince of Wales had played, unless the social ostracism was lifted.

Charles Beresford's threat could not have come at a worse time since another scandal involving Albert Edward was already becoming public knowledge. This was the Tranby Croft Affair, sparked off when Sir William Gordon-Cumming, despite his income of £80,000 a year, was discovered cheating at cards. The Prince of Wales was party to the game and when the matter came into open court the revelation that the heir to the throne took part in gambling sessions in country houses did his reputation infinite harm. If the Beresford Affair had exploded at the same time his position in the country would have been pretty nearly untenable. Certainly his mother felt 'the Monarchy almost is in danger'.

The Beresfords made the most of the Prince's dilemma, Lady Charles's sister even going so far as to write and circulate a pamphlet entitled *Lady River*. Lord Salisbury, now Prime

Minister, was drawn in and warned of 'several people who want to make use of the story in the next General Election for purposes of their own'. Lord Charles, having, it appears, struck the Prince of Wales in a private interview, was on the verge of calling a press conference, with incalculable consequences, when Salisbury at last managed to sort matters out. He arranged an exchange of letters in which the Prince declared he had never intended to distress Lady Charles. And it was agreed that for some time to come it would be Lady Brooke herself who was excluded from royal invitations and fashionable society.

The effects of the Beresford row were still being felt many years later. For though the Prince of Wales was persuaded to shake Lord Charles's hand again in 1897 there was, not unnaturally, never any warmth in their relationship. This had important repercussions after Albert Edward became Edward VII. As King he found the Royal Navy riven in two by the extreme violence of the disagreement between Beresford, representing the conservative view in the navy, and Sir John Fisher who, apprehensive of Germany's intentions, was anxious for rapid modernisation. Though the King's own inclinations were towards reform, what would have happened if Beresford had remained his friend? In the event, when Fisher felt inclined to throw in the towel it was royal support that encouraged him to stay on and see his plans through. In consequence, when war came in 1914, Britain had a navy ready to meet all that Germany had built up.

In spite of the initial difficulties Albert Edward's life throughout most of the 1890s continued to be dominated by his friendship with Lady Brooke, or the Countess of Warwick as she became when her husband succeeded his father. Altogether the Prince, who was twenty years her senior, remained on close terms with her for nine years. Before long it was accepted in the society in which he moved that she was to be invited to the same London receptions and the same country-house weekends as he was. Easton Lodge, her country house in Essex, became a favourite retreat of his, and the fact that Lord Warwick remained on good terms with him helped retain the cloak of respectability.

Lady Warwick was later to describe the Prince as 'a very perfect gentle lover'. She herself had serious shortcomings.

Not for nothing was she known as 'Babbling Brooke' – the Tranby Croft Affair is said to have come out into the open because of her loose tongue. The Princess of Wales, though normally tolerant, could not stand her. It was regarded as highly significant that, after Lady Brooke had triggered off the Beresford Affair, Alexandra saw fit to remain abroad during her husband's fiftieth birthday celebrations. And though the Prince might say 'the Princess has been an angel of goodness throughout all this, but then she is a lady, and could never do anything that was mean or small', the Princess never did trust Daisy. It took the tragic death of their eldest son, the weak and dissipated Albert Victor to whom Albert Edward had been such a bad example, to bring the married couple fully together again.

The Princess continued to look askance at the permanent fascination which Paris exercised over her husband. Her suspicions were justified more than she ever knew. Many years later Christopher Hibbert studied these visits through the records of the Paris Prefecture of Police. Though the Prince went 'incognito' as Duke of Lancaster or Earl of Chester, everyone knew who he was and he was given police protection and kept under close surveillance.

> He had made indefatigable attempts to give the slip to French detectives who followed him everywhere . . . but generally they managed to keep up with him and were able to submit reports of meetings with celebrated beauties in the Jardin des Plantes, of long afternoons spent with intimate friends, the Comtesse Edmond de Pourtales in the rue Tronchet, the Baronne Alphonse de Rothschild in the Faubourg St. Honoré and the Princesse de Sagan on the corner of the Esplanade des Invalides.
> The police watched him on his visits to Mme Kauchine, a Russian beauty who rented a room in the Hotel du Rhin; to 'the widow Signoret', mistress of the Duc de Rohan; to a certain Dame Verneuil who had an apartment on the second floor at 39 rue Lafayette; to the Baronne de Pilar at the Hotel Choiseul; to Miss Chamberlayne (described in 1884 as his *maîtresse en titre*) at the Hotel Balmoral; to unidentified ladies at the Hotel Cribe and the Hotel Liverpool in the rue de Castiglione. The police had been particularly concerned by his visits to the Hotel du Calais, where he often spent most of the night with a mysterious woman [who turned out to be the Comtesse

de Boutourline, wife of the Prefect of Moscow] ...
The Prince had spent other evenings with the delightful
English courtesan, Catherine Walters [the famous 'Skit-
tles']; had visited his favourite brothel Le Chabalais,
where the chair on which he sat with his chosen young
woman was still displayed over a generation later to the
brothel's customers. He had gone to the Maison Dorée
with the Duc de Gramont to meet degenerate, passionate
and consumptive Giulia Beneni, known as La Barucci
who arrived very late and, on being reprimanded by the
Duke, turned her back on her royal visitor, lifted her
skirts to her waist and said, 'you told me to show him my
best side'. He also asked La Barucci's rival, Cora Pearl,
who had appeared before him naked except for a string of
pearls and a sprig of parsley ...

'*Ullo Wales!*' the dancer La Goulue vulgarly called out to him
at the Moulin Rouge, '*Est-ce que tu vas payer mon cham-
pagne?*' He was happy to pay.

Though at home the Prince of Wales as he grew older was
content to have an affair with one woman at a time, and less
inclined than he had been in his youth to flit from one woman
to another, his ardour for Lady Warwick cooled some years
before their affair ended. Her taste for ostentatious living had
led to attacks in the radical press and this in turn led to her
conversion to socialism, albeit of an odd sort. Her royal lover
found the intensity of her views difficult to bear. The arrival of
another child, not his and therefore proof of her roving
fancies, was taken by him as a suitable occasion to bow out.
This was in 1898, less than three years before he came to the
throne. As usual this Prince of Wales, unlike his famous
predecessor George IV, arranged that the parting was an
amicable one. Indeed he told her that he had shown one of her
letters to his wife. 'She really quite forgives and condones the
past as I have corroborated what you wrote about our friendship having been platonic for some years.' The scheming
Daisy had of course been anxious to clear her name and not to
become a social outcast after her royal lover gave her up. She
continued to seek friendly relations with royalty, but Alexandra kept her at arm's length. In the new reign Lady Warwick
even tried her hand at influencing her former lover politically
until a firm message was sent from Alexandra telling her to
desist as her efforts were causing comment of the wrong sort.

The troubles Lady Warwick brought in her wake were not to end there. Though a socialist and an early supporter of the Labour Party she remained as extravagant and unbusinesslike as she had been in her heyday. Having eaten deeply into her capital and become financially embarrassed to the tune of £100,000, with the help of that seedy journalist Frank Harris she let it be known after her royal lover's death that she planned to restore her finances by publishing his love letters. This was a thinly disguised form of blackmail. Again, Albert Edward had failed to follow the advice of his friend Rosa Lewis: 'No letters, no lawyers, and kiss my baby's bottom.' It was seen at once that such a publication from its modes of address alone, written to 'My own adored little Daisy wife' and signed 'Your only love', would be dynamite. Once again Albert Edward's indiscreet letters to a lady friend threatened to undermine the monarchy. On the grounds that King George V, as his father's heir, held the copyright, the Palace went to law. Quietly and efficiently, an injunction was granted by a judge in chambers forbidding Lady Warwick to proceed. Her blackmail attempt had failed and the story of her efforts remained buried for fifty years.

It was fortunate that the Prince of Wales's affair with his 'Darling Daisy' ended before he came to the throne: scheming, interfering, irresponsible Lady Warwick as the King's mistress at the heart of affairs would have been a highly dangerous phenomenon. Albert Edward was lucky, too, that within a matter of weeks of his final break with her he met her successor at Sandown Races. Mrs George Keppel was eminently more suitable than her predecessor to be a king's mistress. Not only was she beautiful and charming but she had intelligence, vivacity and humour as well. She combined a respectable social background, which had been Mrs Langtry's weak point, with a discretion which Lady Warwick so sadly lacked.

Alice Keppel was the daughter of an admiral and wife of the younger son of an earl (a descendant of William III's male favourite). As the Keppels' daughter has pointed out, married life had not been easy: 'He was one of ten, and she of nine, children, and at the time of their marriage beauty and charm had been their main dowry'. The Honourable George Keppel was, like the Earl of Warwick, an extremely tolerant and understanding man with whom, both as Prince of Wales and King, Albert Edward remained on good terms. Even when he had to take a job to help his wife to keep up with the expense of her high life he was uncomplaining. (Many years later, when Mrs Keppel had bought an Italian villa with money the King had left her, her husband was to receive the final indignity of being pointed out by the slightly muddled locals as *l'ultimo amante della Regina Victoria*.)

The Prince was a rapidly ageing gourmet and roué of fifty-six when he first met his new love. She was twenty-nine about the same age as his daughters, but there was a vast difference between her grace and self-assurance and those dowdy, dull and painfully shy princesses. In addition to her fine figure – in keeping with the tastes of the era, if tending to plumpness with the passing of the years – she had a finely moulded face surmounted by a luxuriant head of chestnut hair. Above all she had a quiet dignity and inner strength. 'What spirit, wit and resilience that woman has,' remarked Princess Daisy of Pless. With a deep, animated voice, Mrs Keppel was an excellent conversationalist who took care to be well informed. 'One of the secrets of her success,' declared Harold Nicolson who knew her in later years, 'was that she could be amusing without malice; she never repeated a cruel witticism.' 'I never heard her repeat an unkind word of anybody,' echoed Lord Hardinge of Penshurst.

As her lover grew older, and presumably his sensual needs became less, Alice Keppel's main role came to be to amuse and entertain him, to ward off his fiery temper, and above all to prevent him from being bored. 'He likes to join in general conversation, interjecting remarks,' she once told an acquaintance, 'but he prefers to listen rather than to talk himself.' Alice was to be relied on to keep a conversation going, though she had sensitivity enough to know when silence was called for. It became almost obligatory to invite her to any party the Prince was to attend, certainly if he was to be kept in a good humour. To exclude her or snub her in any way was to invite a downpour of royal wrath.

In the main the still-beautiful Alexandra approved of Mrs Keppel. 'Queen Alexandra was very fond of her and encouraged the liaison,' says Princess Alice of Battenberg, especially as Mrs Keppel 'never flaunted herself or took advantage of her

150

position as King's favourite'. The long-suffering wife, by now almost totally deaf, recognised the necessity for her husband to have a female friend, and she found this lady more congenial and tactful than her predecessor. 'What do you think of that charming Lady Warwick,' she was to ask during the General Election of 1906, 'mounting a waggon at the corner of the street and addressing her comrades?' Alice Keppel could be relied on never to do that. Still, Alexandra was only human, and the over-frequent presence of Mrs Keppel was apt to spoil what little time she still enjoyed with her husband. During a happy family get-together at Cowes Regatta one year the future George V reported to his wife 'Mrs K arrives tomorrow . . . and I am afraid peace and quiet will not remain'. And Alexandra, who retained her own youthful figure, was unable to resist loud laughter at the sight of her fat husband and his, by now ample, mistress squeezed together in a carriage.

Mrs Keppel's position became one of some importance when, on the death of Queen Victoria, Albert Edward, at the age of fifty-nine, at last came into his own as King Edward VII, 'Edward the Caresser' as Henry James disparagingly dubbed him. Though the new King surrounded himself with a number of male friends, including Lord Esher and the millionaire financier Ernest Cassel, he still needed feminine company. As he became older and his political worries increased, as his temper became more easily aroused, and as the threshold of his boredom got progressively lower, so Alice Keppel's soothing company became the balm which was essential to keep him going with any degree of comfort to himself and those around him. Her beauty, charm, good temper and circumspection exactly suited his needs, needs now of the spirit more than the body.

Though the new reign cleared away some of the cobwebs that had surrounded Queen Victoria, to the public at large existing moral codes remained. Conventions still had to be abided by: sinning was acceptable only if never found out. There was, therefore, considerable admiration from those in the know at the aplomb with which, behind the façade, the King quietly carried on his previous way of life. (To accommodate his close female acquaintances he even had special accommodation – dubbed 'the King's loose box' – provided

151

for them in Westminster Abbey at his Coronation.) In this the press was his ally. King Edward's flair for the more flamboyant aspects of monarchy, his almost theatrical feeling for ceremonial, and the prestige which his foreign visits and influence were thought to bring his country, together with his obvious bonhomie and his widely-shared interest in the turf, ensured his tremendous popularity. This popularity, combined with the reverence with which, due to Queen Victoria, the throne was now regarded, meant that as long as the King did not parade his attachment to Mrs Keppel too openly, he was assured that British newspapers would not draw attention to her. Some people, including his strait-laced nephew the Kaiser, wondered at his ability to get away with it. The German Emperor and the German press were not prepared to turn a blind eye to Mrs Keppel's existence, and the Kaiser's criticism of his uncle's relationship with her – something which German newspapers were also prone to highlight – did nothing to improve the already strained relations between the British and German monarchs. Even so, when he was in England, the Kaiser thought it wise to cultivate the King's friend.

Among those in Britain in a position to know the facts, Mrs Keppel was accepted as an influence for good. There was never any criticism or suspicion of the type which had, for instance, surrounded Queen Victoria's Indian servant and adviser Abdul Karim, 'the Munshi', in the 1890s. 'It would have been difficult,' says Lord Hardinge, 'to have found another lady who would have filled the part of friend to King Edward with the same loyalty and discretion.' Luckily her politics were not of the extreme sort favoured by Lady Warwick. She was in fact liberal in outlook. That she had a social conscience was borne out by the way she forced Lord Alington to take her on a drive to Hoxton where she wished to show him the slum property he owned. Knowing Mrs Keppel's quiet influence, her well-informed mind, good sense and utter trustworthiness, Government ministers found her a useful vehicle for conducting business. For while the power of the Crown to determine events was very much circumscribed by this time, the uncertainty of the King's temper and his strong views on certain subjects often made him a difficult man with whom to deal. Lloyd George, for one, made a point of becoming one of Alice Keppel's wide circle of friends, and she was to be a periodic guest at 10 Downing Street when Asquith was Prime Minister, as well as at the home of the Winston Churchills. Later Lord Hardinge, who was Under Secretary of State for Foreign Affairs at the time, was also to reveal: 'There were one of two occasions when the King was in disagreement with the Foreign Office, and I was able, through her, to advise the King with a view to the policy of the Government being accepted.' She was a valuable emollient in the relations between King and Government in this far from easy decade, her standing being enhanced by the fact that she was known to be 'very loyal to the King, and patriotic at the same time,' and that she 'never utilised her knowledge to her own advantage, or to that of her friends'.

The knowledge she did acquire was used to maximum advantage. Not only was she useful in government and diplomatic circles in putting certain viewpoints to the King, but she also culled information from those circles and transmitted it back to him and, where appropriate, his ministers. Foreign ambassadors whispering in her ear at country-house parties were apt to find that the views they expressed were quickly passed on, as when the Austrian Ambassador, having discussed the Bosnian crisis with 'la Favourita Keppel', found his remarks next day in the possession of the Foreign Secretary. It is curious that, at a time when women under Mrs Pankhurst were seeking so violently and flamboyantly to acquire political influence through the suffragette movement, Mrs Keppel was exercising far more influence than any of them behind the scenes as a domestic go-between and peacemaker.

The King's most curious friendship in these years was with Agnes Keyser who was seventeen years older than Alice Keppel and who devoted her life to running a nursing home for officers. He called on her and dined with her as a quiet escape from formality. She fed him well, mothered him and possibly dosed him, but any sexual relationship appears unlikely. Even in Mrs Keppel's case the Archbishop of Canterbury, having been placed next to her at dinner, came to the conclusion that this was Edward's way of saying that the relationship between them, in these later years at least, was platonic.

It is quite possible that he made up for this during the *en*

153

garçon visits he made to Marienbad each year of his reign. At this Bohemian spa women the royal private secretary, Frederick Ponsonby, described as having a 'murky past' were much in evidence. Ponsonby was even approached there by a demi-mondaine who had travelled from Vienna 'to have the honour of sleeping with the King'. 'Being told this was out of the question, she said if it came to the worst she would sleep with me so that she should not waste the money spent on her ticket.' The highly respectable Liberal Prime Minister, Henry Campbell-Bannerman, was distressed to find Marienbad filled with 'an extraordinary number of painted ladies' and at the spectacle of a monarch 'recklessly abandoned to the society of a few semi-déclassé ladies and men to match'. One young girl was puzzled by the eager preparations at her hotel when the King was coming to tea with one of his lady friends: scent was sprayed everywhere and the curtains closed though it was broad daylight. Right to the end of his life, at Marienbad King Edward was able to entertain female acquaintances at dinner at his hotel, or at tea at theirs, or on drives in the woods.

Regular annual visits were also paid to Biarritz, this time with Mrs Keppel for company. The King often went first to Paris while she, usually accompanied by her children (never by her long-suffering husband), made her way across France treated like royalty by the railway authorities. To preserve appearances she did not stay with the King but took over Ernest Cassel's Villa Eugenie. For three weeks, in March and April, they relaxed by the sea or in the surrounding countryside. It so happened that Asquith became Prime Minister during one of these sojourns. In the King's mind there was no question of returning to England. The busy Asquith had to make the slow journey out to Biarritz for the formality of kissing hands. Though his enforced excursion provoked widespread criticism at home, none of the newspapers divulged the fact that Mrs Keppel's presence helped keep the King out there. Two years later, in the spring of 1910, the weather at what Queen Alexandra called 'that horrid Biarritz' was bad, but the King's proneness to follow habit meant that once again, in spite of the bronchitis that was killing him, he was unwilling to cut short his stay there with Mrs Keppel. Had he given way to the Queen's pleas and gone with Alexandra to the Mediterranean his life might have been prolonged.

His deterioration after his return to England was swift. When he collapsed, Queen Alexandra rushed home to be with him. Realising that he had an appointment to see her rival, with typical self-effacement she sent for Mrs Keppel to come before it was too late. She was one of his last friends to see him alive. After his death the Queen appeared to hover over the body as if to demonstrate that now, perhaps for the first time, it was all hers; despite everything, she consoled herself, he had always loved her best of all. With his death, the light had gone out of her life and she was to spend her remaining years a broken figure. Life changed for others as well. 'Nothing will ever be quite the same again,' George Keppel told his young daughter. 'Life with all its joys,' Alice herself confessed, 'have come to a full stop at least for me.' She was to have some consolation in finding that her lover had made financial provision for her.

The King's death was mourned by millions, most of whom knew little of his way of life but probably guessed a good deal. It was left to Sir John Fisher to give what is perhaps the most apt summing up of this wayward and self-confident monarch – 'How *human* he was. He could sin "as it were with a cart-rope", and yet could be loved the more for it!'

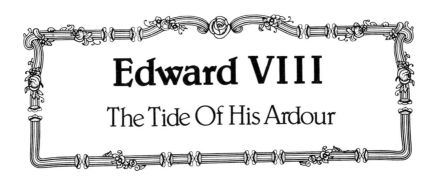

Edward VIII

The Tide Of His Ardour

Twenty-six years after the death of Edward VII, a white-haired woman, very erect and extremely dignified, was heard in the dining room of London's Ritz Hotel pronouncing on the latest royal crisis. The woman was Alice Keppel speaking on the abdication of the old King's grandson, Edward VIII, who insisted on marrying a woman rather than keeping a mistress. Things had indeed come a long way since old Edward's day.

The young man in question had first become a focus of public attention as the new heir to the throne when he appeared at the funeral of his grandfather. Ironically, had Edward VII lived longer he would probably have had a much greater rapport with this young prince than the boy's own father. But as the meteor-like brilliance of the Edwardian era quickly died away it was replaced by the plodding respectability which was for twenty-five years to distinguish the reign of George V. Except for a rumour, scotched by a court action at the time of his accession, that he had married a naval officer's daughter before his marriage to Queen Mary, no breath of scandal ever touched this George's name. He was a faithful if undemonstrative husband who had been extremely close to his father but who then lamentably reverted to the Hanoverian tradition of being unable to build up an understanding relationship with his own heir. In this lay the seeds of tragedy. King George was a hard taskmaster, given to naval brusqueness, with little ability to understand young people. A Victorian to the core, he fought a running battle against many aspects of the twentieth century. It was perhaps partly in retaliation that his eldest son felt the need to epitomise all things modern.

The gulf between the generations widened with the coming of the 1914 War when the Prince of Wales was twenty. Slim, inexperienced and shy, he fought hard to get as near to the trenches as officialdom would allow. When the four-year holocaust ended he emerged as a popular figure, identified with the younger generation, and with an ability to project himself to all classes of people. At this stage of his life it would undoubtedly have been best for him, personally, to have been left to resume what there was of family life, to put down roots and seek out for himself a suitable wife, as other men who had survived that terrible war were seeking to do. This was not allowed him. At the behest of Lloyd George, then Prime Minister, he was launched on a series of tours to spread the message of monarchy and unity to the four corners of the British Empire. He succeeded brilliantly. His boyish good looks and his affability raised the prestige of the Crown and of the heir apparent to unprecedented heights. Meanwhile, behind the smile and the acclaim, those associated with him were worried by a basic loneliness, black moods, stubbornness and occasional lapses from good behaviour.

One reason for the Prince's moods was the fact that he was absent from London at a time when he had already established an intimate female friendship there. During the early part of the War he had started to set what was to prove to be a pattern by developing a passion for Lady Coke who was not only older than he was but already married. Near the end of the War a more permanent relationship began. During a Zeppelin raid a young woman walking through Belgrave Square ran for shelter into a house where he was attending a dance. She was Mrs Dudley Ward, again older than he and already married to a Member of Parliament from whom she soon separated. Mrs Ward had charm, intelligence and fearlessness, all traits the Prince admired. She was not beautiful but petite and attractive, again the type he preferred. Gone was the Edwardian taste, typified by Mrs Keppel, for rounded matronly figures. This Edward preferred the boyish flat-bosomed type which blossomed in the 1920s.

The Prince of Wales's friendship with Mrs Dudley Ward,

though its intensity declined with the passage of time, lasted altogether for sixteen years, up to his fortieth birthday. By coincidence, she was related by marriage to Lord Esher who had played a key role as a royal confidant in the reign of Edward VII. 'Be discreet like Mrs Keppel,' Esher advised her. Mrs Ward could not have been more discreet. Though she was to obtain a divorce from her husband, she never had any thought of marrying the Prince of Wales. She was well aware of what was acceptable and what was not. She knew that, with the fall of so many European thrones during the War, a wider choice of bride would be allowed the heir to the throne, but that a divorced commoner was in no way acceptable.

In any case her affection for the Prince did not match his passion and, for some years, utter devotion to her. Her conduct during those years helped to ensure that the knowledge of their relationship was limited to London society. She also provided an anchor for him between those exhausting and disorientating world tours. Nevertheless the Prince of Wales's affair with a married woman, to the great distress of his parents, prevented the normal processes from taking place whereby the heir to the throne sought out a suitable bride and contracted an acceptable marriage. In this respect Mrs Ward performed the same unfortunate function for the future Edward VIII that Mrs Fitzherbert had performed for the future George IV.

Like George IV, this Prince did not remain faithful to his principal inamorata. His future wife was to admit 'he had a lot of girls before me'. Throughout his tours abroad rumours persisted of passing affairs, of his unaccounted disappearance from time to time, and at least one royal bastard. 'Indeed,' says one of his biographers, 'during the whole of his youth the Prince was criticised for his over-indulgence in the sexual act.' A 1928 Kenya safari, for instance, 'was sometimes brought to a halt for several days, while the Prince indulged in a light-hearted fancy'. During at least part of this Kenya tour his newest London friend, Thelma, Viscountess Furness, was in attendance and her candid memoirs were later to talk of 'his arms about me . . . his words of love . . . the mounting tide of his ardour'.

Lady Furness, formerly Thelma Vanderbilt, was another married woman. She had already had one divorce and was now married to a husband considerably older than herself. With her painted rosebud mouth, she was quite a good-looking woman noted for her dry sense of humour, and generally well-liked. She had another attribute which the Prince found attractive. She was American, and Americans with their free-and-easy and up-to-date ways always seemed to appeal to him. After all, he prided himself on being thoroughly modern, and this reflected itself both in his choice of friends and his love of night-life. As so commonly happened among those who had survived the War, and could afford it, in his private hours he threw himself into a life of pleasure. Lady Furness, highly sociable as she was, helped fill these hours.

But as the Prince advanced into his thirties, his boyish looks still reflecting a certain immaturity, and as his brothers one by one began to get married, there was growing evidence that there was another, more domestic side to his nature still awaiting satisfaction. His home-making proclivities were only partly catered for when his father gave him Fort Belvedere, an eighteenth-century fantasy of a fort on the edge of Windsor Great Park. His future wife was to find in him 'a deep loneliness, an overtone of spiritual isolation'. Still he made no effort to seek permanent companionship through marriage. Any appreciation he may have had of his duty as heir to the throne to marry was exceeded by his horror of arranged and loveless matches. As he made clear to his friend Walter Monckton, he had no time for 'a marriage blessed by the bishops . . . in which the two spouses . . . went their separate ways *sub rosa*'. Unfortunately he never did meet a suitable unmarried girl with whom he fell in love. So he made do with relationships outside marriage.

It was probably late in 1930, when he was thirty-six, that Lady Furness introduced him to another American married woman, Wallis Simpson. Mrs Simpson, who came from a family of long standing in Baltimore, had married, when she was twenty, a flying-officer in the United States Navy. She called him 'the world's most fascinating aviator' but it turned out he was addicted to the bottle. Following a separation and an unsuccessful reconciliation she obtained a divorce after eleven years of marriage. Eight months later, about the time the Prince of Wales was on amorous safari in Kenya, she married Ernest Simpson who was a British subject. They settled in London where he had business interests, and built up a circle of friends largely of American origin, including Lady Furness and her sister. Hence the eventual introduction to the Prince of Wales.

There was no question of love at first sight. Though the lady admitted to being 'mesmerised' by the acquaintance, for a long time the Prince appeared hardly to notice her, and encounters were rare. Then gradually she and her husband became part of his inner circle. Here Lady Furness still reigned supreme. Early in 1934, however, she arranged a two-month visit to America and before leaving suggested to Mrs Simpson that she 'look after' the Prince. When she returned it was to discover that 'Wallis took my advice all too literally'. The Prince of Wales now began keeping Lady Furness – who according to the newspapers had been associating with Prince Aly Khan in her absence – at arm's length. At the same time he abruptly terminated his long-standing links with Mrs Dudley Ward – by giving instructions to his telephone operator not to put through her calls.

On the brink of his fortieth birthday the future king had fallen more passionately in love than ever before. To understand the events of the next three years it is necessary to recognise what Walter Monckton was to call 'the intensity and depth of his devotion to her'. 'To him she was the perfect woman . . . his lonely nature found in her a spiritual companionship.' At this stage, at least, Mrs Simpson appears not to have been affected in the same way. 'My impression is that for a long time she remained unaffected by my interest,' says her future husband. She was however exhilarated by the experience, by the 'aura of power and authority', as many before her over the centuries had been at capturing the heir to the throne. There were the more obvious attractions of expensive gifts and jewellery. ('Her collection of jewels is the talk of London,' Chips Channon tells us in his diary, and it has been suggested that one reason for the famous flight of her solicitor to her later hideout in Cannes was to seek the return to the royal collection of Queen Alexandra's emeralds that her suitor was thought to have given her.) Even more important was the fact that the Prince was 'the open sesame to a new and glittering world'. In fashionable London society 'I became aware of a rising curiosity concerning me, of new doors opening'.

Mrs Simpson cannot be blamed for her failure, in the early stages of this relationship, to think matters through to their logical conclusion. 'Throughout history,' Edward's biographer Frances Donaldson points out, 'the favourite of the King has been regarded as an honourable position and only few women have dared to look beyond it.' Without a doubt it was Edward who encouraged this favourite to look further. Such behaviour on his part can only be explained by the fact that he was completely obsessed by her and that his relationship with her became the only thing in life that mattered to him.

What can explain this obsession? Certainly there must have been physical attraction. Whilst not a regular beauty, Mrs Simpson was an attractive if rather angular woman with an indefinable chic and impeccable taste to make up for any lack of classical features. Added to this was her conversational ability, her liveliness and outspokenness and her dry sense of humour. Again, she had an independence of spirit and a directness linked with what she called 'my wholly American outlook'. Then she interested herself in the Prince, his life and his troubles – 'I listened, and I sympathised, and I understood'. Finally, she had the domestic qualities – she was a good homemaker. Some people may say that with all this went a wish to dominate, and a readiness on his part to be dominated, but this side of her could also be seen as providing the maternal qualities which his mother had lacked. Whatever its cause, the air of possessiveness which she developed offended his family and helped build a wall around him which became increasingly difficult to scale. Even his closest brother, the Duke of Kent, was convinced he was bewitched.

Mrs Simpson has revealed that it was in the summer of 1934 that 'we crossed the line that makes the indefinable boundary between friendship and love'. As regards her feelings, the observant Cecil Beaton was to have his doubts. 'She loves him,' he suggested, 'but I fear she is not in love with him.' No close observer could have such reservations about the Prince. We have since learned from Walter Monckton that it was again in 1934 that Edward made up his mind that Wallis Simpson was the woman in his life and that he would not be content to have her as his mistress. By hook or by crook he would marry her. It soon became clear to George V also that what he called his son's 'latest friendship' was something out of the ordinary, and well might Mrs Simpson have a 'premonitory shiver' as she felt the King's eyes resting on her while she danced with his heir at the Silver Jubilee Ball in 1935. Lady Airlie has recorded one of the old King's last outbursts: 'I pray to God that my eldest son will never marry and have children, and that nothing will come between Bertie and Lilibet and the throne.' He was nearer the truth than he ever knew when he told his Prime Minister, Stanley Baldwin, 'After I am dead the boy will ruin himself in twelve months'.

Though the boy never discussed the affair with his father, by the closing stages of the old King's life the situation had drifted into extremely dangerous waters. On the one hand, the Prince of Wales abjectly worshipped Mrs Simpson and was obstinately determined to raise her status as high as he could. She, on her part, was a foreigner with little knowledge of British customs outside the life of a brilliant social set. Certainly the nuances of the constitution were beyond her, and she did not fully realise that her record of two marriages ending in divorce would present an insuperable obstacle to her acceptability as her admirer's wife. No such excuse could be offered for the Prince. His lifetime's experience at the centre of British public life should have taught him that, even at this stage in the twentieth century, the vast majority of people outside the brittle society in which he was at home would not tolerate the marriage of the heir to the throne, however popular and dashing he might be, to a double divorcée. He liked to think such narrow views were limited to his father's court and to the ecclesiastical hierarchy. His view that most people, especially the younger generation, were on his side turned out to be a grave misreading of public opinion, both in Britain and in the self-governing Dominions, in the 1930s. That Mrs Simpson was a commoner, and an American to boot, would have been hard enough for some to swallow. Nevertheless, had she been Miss Wallis Warfield from Baltimore, although some heads would have shaken, Edward would, as King, in all probability have had his way.

It was now almost a hundred years since Queen Victoria's accession had helped to transform the standing of the monarchy. In his reign of twenty-five years George V had raised its popularity still further by his example as a family man. What his successor overlooked was the fact that, though the powers of the Crown had shrunk almost to insignificance, its influence as an example of family life and moral rectitude was by now one of its most important features. Marriage of the monarch to a divorced woman could not form part of such an equation.

Edward VIII

Make Mrs Simpson His Mistress

The crisis advanced a stage further in January 1936 when George V, worn out and dejected, was gathered to his fathers. The new King, now Edward VIII, already in his own words 'caught up in an inner conflict', was raised to the rarified atmosphere of the throne. He later said he wanted to be king but on his own terms, 'a King in a modern way'. This he vaguely defined as wanting to 'let in some fresh air' on the monarchy, which in effect appears to have meant little more than reducing the ceremonial and majestic elements of the institution and putting greater emphasis on informality. To his old friend Walter Monckton he confided 'they must take him as he was... available for public business... but his private life was to be his own'. As regards the most time-consuming side of public business, the continual hard grind of reading State Papers, his initial enthusiasm quickly waned. Perhaps unfortunately, his interest centred on foreign affairs, and here his pro-German stance alarmed those who heard of it, his Conservative ministers as well as members of the Labour Opposition. Simpson influence was of course looked for but not detected, though she was to accompany him in his foreign activities in Germany and elsewhere in the years immediately after his abdication.

As regards the private life King Edward said he wanted to retain, this did not mean he intended keeping quiet his friendship with Mrs Simpson. The august columns of the Court Circular, at his behest, deliberately chronicled the comings and goings of his circle of personal friends including Mr and Mrs Ernest Simpson. As Edward later explained to Baldwin, 'the lady is my friend and I do not wish to let her in by the back door, but quite openly'. This was clearly to be no repetition of the age-old phenomenon of the royal mistress. It was, according to Mrs Simpson, shortly before a dinner party to which the Simpsons were invited together with the Baldwins that the King told her in specific terms what his intention was: 'Sooner or later my Prime Minister must meet my future wife.'

With such intentions, timing soon became important. The Coronation was fixed for May 1937. Though the established Church of England could trace its origins to Henry VIII's wish to divorce Catherine of Aragon, it now stood firmly against divorce and, as Edward himself later pointed out, 'for me to have gone through a Coronation ceremony while harbouring in my heart a secret intention to marry contrary to the Church's tenets would have meant being crowned with a lie on my lips'. Apparently he would not have minded being crowned having already married contrary to the Church's tenets. The upshot of this was that 'I was determined before I would think of being crowned to settle once and for all the question of my right to marry'. The way in which he chose to 'settle' this was to maintain complete silence till Mrs Simpson had obtained a divorce.

Was it necessary that the affair should proceed in this way at all? It has been suggested by a friend of the Simpsons that it was the King who, because of his jealousy of her husband, pressed Mrs Simpson to seek a divorce. 'But for the King's obstinacy the affair would have run its course without breaking up the Simpsons' marriage.' There have been varying suggestions concerning Ernest Simpson's attitude to his wife's admirer, including the joke about his saying 'My only regret is that I have but one wife to lay down for my king'. Certainly he showed great forbearance until his cohabitation with his wife was no longer required. With regard to Mrs Simpson herself, she says that she had grave doubts as to the possibility of what the new King was now proposing. 'The idea is impossible . . . they'd never let you,' she says she told him when he first spelt out his intentions. Thereafter she obviously agreed to go along with him in clearing the way.

The first step along the road was in fact taken by Ernest Simpson when he moved out of the marital home shortly after the Simpson-Baldwin dinner in late May. This caused alarm in some quarters. As Winston Churchill pointed out, 'Mr Simpson was a safeguard'. According to his wife he had found 'a new emotional centre for his life' (presumably Mary Kirk Raffray whom he later married) but, if so, this was obviously some time after she had found her own emotional centre. Nevertheless it was he who provided grounds for divorce by being discovered in a hotel bed with a lady named Buttercup Kennedy. Though there is no evidence to prove that he deliberately arranged to be found in a compromising situation with Miss Kennedy for his wife's convenience, divorce by collusion – with the innocent husband doing the 'decent thing' by being found in bed with 'another woman' – was quite common at the time.

The King now set about assisting Mrs Simpson with her divorce arrangements without breathing a word to his ministers. Walter Monckton surmised that his reason for this was recognition that 'if anyone in his service sufficiently clearly realised what he wanted to do, his plans would probably be frustrated'. To Monckton, and anyone else involved, his explanation of his interest was 'He didn't see why Mrs Simpson should stay tied to an unhappy marriage simply because she was his friend'. Mrs Simpson kept up a similar pretence, misleading her friends with phrases like 'There is no question of marriage', 'Of course not', 'She would never marry the King', right up to the eve of the abdication.

In contrast to this secrecy about ultimate intentions was the manner in which the King publicly flaunted his friendship, as if he was trying to get people used to the idea of such a partnership. To Churchill, for instance, he made it clear that 'he was not ashamed of his friendship, and he was not going to hide it or try to deceive people'! That August, with Mrs Simpson and a number of other friends, he went on a Mediterranean cruise in the yacht *Nahlin*, pursued by the world press. American newspapers, in full cry over 'Queen Wally', dubbed it 'the best story since the Resurrection'. This of course put growing pressure on the British Press, which had hitherto maintained total silence over the affair, on the basis that the monarchy had for many years been so dignified and above controversy as to deserve restrained treatment.

That autumn Mrs Simpson removed herself to a house in Suffolk, where the hearing of her divorce case was set down for 27 October. A week before the hearing, however, there occurred what the King called 'an intervention from an unexpected quarter'. Since the intervention was from the Prime Minister, Edward's surprise shows what an unreal world he had been living in. Whilst it was true that the Royal Marriages Act did not apply to the King himself, nevertheless, by 1936, the powers of the Crown were so circumscribed that no monarch could contemplate matrimony without his Government's consent. No one could accuse Baldwin of rushing things. He had for some time been under pressure to act – from Cabinet colleagues, from members of the King's Household and not least from disgusted Britons abroad sending him sheaves of foreign newspaper cuttings. For long he hesitated. He entertained benevolent, almost fatherly feelings towards the King and was prepared to turn a blind eye for months. But, like Edward's Private Secretary, he was aware that his ultimate responsibility was towards the institution of monarchy rather than the man who at the time happened to be monarch.

Fortifying himself with a glass of whisky, and speaking with considerable circumspection, Baldwin put the matter in context by pointing to the fact that though royal power had declined 'people expect more of their King than they did a hundred years ago'. Fearful that the divorce proceedings would break the log-jam of press silence, with catastrophic results to the standing of the Crown, he asked 'Cannot the coming divorce be put off?' To this the King, 'doing my best to hide my feelings', as he later admitted, gave his stock reply: 'That is the lady's private business. I have no right to interfere with the private affairs of an individual.' Years later Mrs Simpson blandly admitted that this put-off was 'an attempt to avoid a head-on collision with the Government at this delicate juncture'. The Prime Minister did not presume to ask his Sovereign outright whether he intended marriage. He did however utter a warning: 'I don't believe you can go on like this and get away with it.'

Though the King retained his apparent equanimity in front of Mrs Simpson – 'I am sure I can fix things' – he was a worried man. With the American papers baying like bloodhounds he knew that in Fleet Street there was 'terrific pressure building up' to break the story and perhaps to jeopardise the chances of the divorce going through. So while on the one hand he was telling his Prime Minister that he had 'no right to interfere with the private affairs of an individual', on the other hand he was seeking an interview with a leading press baron, Lord Beaverbrook, and asking him to use his influence with other newspaper proprietors to ensure that the divorce proceedings were reported just as any other divorce might be. Beaverbrook was the man whom his arch-enemy Baldwin had described as seeking 'power without responsibility – the prerogative of the harlot throughout the ages'. Though later Beaverbrook boasted that he had got involved in abdication intrigue 'to bugger Baldwin', on this occasion he had the wool pulled over his eyes, accepting at face value the royal argument that it would be wrong to over-publicise someone's divorce simply because she was a friend of the King. No allusion was made to marriage, and Beaverbrook simply assumed that Mrs Simpson was another in the long tradition of Mrs Keppel and those before her. In this spirit he persuaded his press colleagues to carry out the King's wishes. In retrospect it might be thought that the newspapers' policy of restraint was wholly mistaken, since it prevented the build-up of the crisis from becoming known to the British public early enough for the King's delusions to be shattered before it was too late to pull back. Not that, obstinate and obsessed as he was, he was likely to have pulled back.

Though the King might regard the successful granting of a decree nisi to Mrs Simpson with a sense of relief, others closely involved saw it in a different light. To them it transformed an indiscreet friendship, or even a traditional king-mistress relationship, into a potential constitutional crisis. The pressures on Baldwin grew. 'When I was a little boy in Worcestershire reading history books,' he now mused, 'I never thought I should have to interfere between a king and his mistress.' The dangers of the dam of press silence breaking ruled out delay. It was after discussing the whole affair with the Prime Minister that Alexander Hardinge, the King's Private Secretary, whose duty it was to keep his ear close to the ground, warned his master in a letter on 13 November that the silence of the newspapers was 'not going to be maintained' and begged him to send Mrs Simpson abroad. Though roused to fury by what he considered to be Hardinge's 'impertinence', Edward was now under no illusion that he could drift into marriage. The letter provoked him into arranging an audience with Baldwin to make it clear 'that if, as would now appear, he and the Government are against my marrying Mrs Simpson, I am prepared to go'.

Baldwin came to this audience having taken various soundings of opinion which confirmed his own instincts. It was therefore with conviction that he made clear, 'I believe I know what the British people will tolerate and what they would not'. As the King's wife would automatically become queen, and successor to the spotless reputations of Queen Alexandra and Queen Mary, he made it clear that public opinion would not tolerate the marriage of the monarch to the twice-divorced Mrs Simpson. For the first time Edward was equally frank, expressing his determination to marry Mrs Simpson as soon as she was free. The depth of his love was quite apparent. Baldwin was later to declare: 'The King's face at times wore such a look of beauty as might have lighted the face of a young knight who had caught a glimpse of the Holy Grail.'

But for such a knightly attitude, the simplest solution to the problem would have been for him to have installed Mrs Simpson as his mistress, and Baldwin actually hinted at such a course. 'I said to him, was it absolutely necessary that he should *marry* her,' he later recalled. 'In their peculiar circumstances certain things are sometimes permitted to royalty which are not allowed to the ordinary man.' The fact that the Prime Minister had not acted in the affair at all until the impending divorce threatened to enable Mrs Simpson to marry the King appears to confirm the view that, had Ernest Simpson remained in the wings to preserve appearances in the manner of George Keppel, Baldwin would not have attempted to interfere. One of the American consuls in England at the time was to deplore what he called the hypocrisy of many otherwise respectable, people who 'state openly that it would be all right if the King were to follow the example of some other kings, in the past, and make Mrs Simpson his mistress . . . saying almost in the same breath, that the King must set a moral example to his people'. There was indeed an element of hypocrisy in such a solution, but to most of those involved the alternative, the uncharted rocks of abdication, seemed infinitely worse.

Edward himself was later to draw attention to what he described as the 'paradox' in the Baldwin line. 'It seemed to me that if his argument were carried to its logical conclusion, then I should have taken a mistress. A discreet house nearby, a key to a garden door, decorous associations – the relationship might be privately deplored, but it had notable precedents.' Such a course was impossible, as Walter Monckton knew, because of the King's obsession. 'The Crown is only valuable if it would interest *her*,' he noted at the time. 'He must have marriage because then she can be with him always. Therefore he had no wish to form a "Party" who would keep him on the throne and let her be his mistress.' So the King's reply to Baldwin's hint was an immediate 'Oh, there's no question of that. I am going to marry her . . . I can't do my job without her. I am going to marry her, and I will'.

Though for long Edward kept from Mrs Simpson the extent of the danger he was in, by now she, too, was aware of the impending crisis. It would appear, though, that she did not know that Baldwin had suggested she should be his mistress at the crucial audience. If she had known, would she have taken the line of Elizabeth Woodville in the face of Edward IV's ardour: 'I know I am not good enough to be your queen but am I too good to be your mistress'? Possibly not, for the key to an understanding of Mrs Simpson's role during the remainder of the crisis was her overriding desire to keep her suitor on his throne at all costs. Having been carried along by his optimism in the initial stages, she had been made to face reality on hearing how, after receiving Hardinge's letter, Edward was preparing to confront Baldwin and express his willingness to abdicate. Amid tears, she tells us, her reaction to this news was 'It is madness to think, let alone to talk of such a thing'. After Edward's death she explained to Ralph Martin that she had deployed various arguments in an endeavour to deflect him from the course he was on. 'I told him it was too heavy a load for me to carry. I told him the British people were absolutely right in not wanting a divorced woman for a queen. I told him I didn't want to be queen . . . We had terrible arguments about it. But he was a mule.' One of her suggestions appears to have been not dissimilar from what Baldwin had in mind. 'I told him that if he stayed on as king, it wouldn't be the end for us. I could still come and see him and he could still come and see me.' Again, 'We had terrible arguments about it . . .'

Would such a solution have worked? Though on the one hand she is recorded as saying 'all that formality and responsibility' did not attract her to the idea of being queen, on the other hand, anyone who had witnessed her somewhat bossy behaviour with Edward might have doubted her ability to act in a self-effacing manner behind the scenes. It was not a role for which even her best friends might think her naturally cast. In any case, the King would not entertain such an idea, 'He told me he didn't want to be king without me.' His attachment to her was to him the most beautiful thing in the world, and he would not tolerate anything which cheapened or hid their relationship.

While she was looking for ways out of the impending crisis, Mrs Simpson was approached by the son of Lord Rothermere, Esmond Harmsworth, with the suggestion that the answer lay in a morganatic marriage, the old device used by continental royalty whereby a low-born wife did not rank as consort. Edward's maternal grandfather had been the unhappy product of such a marriage. Though it now appears likely that George I had morganatically married the Duchess of Kendal, such marriages were regarded as without precedent in Britain where, whatever one's origins, to marry the monarch was automatically to be raised to royal status. After an initial feeling that the continental device was somewhat 'inhuman', Mrs Simpson came round to the view that the idea was worth trying, and took it up with the King. His first reaction was also one of distaste, but as she was keen to have the possibility investigated he agreed to suggest it to the Prime Minister. 'Is this the sort of thing I've stood for in public life?' Baldwin instinctively asked himself. Nevertheless, when pressed, he agreed to have the proposal formally examined.

The implications of this were profound, for up to this point Baldwin had kept his discussions with the King on an informal basis. Now it was necessary that the marriage be discussed by both the British Government and those of the self-governing Dominions. From this it followed that constitutionally the King must accept whatever advice he was given. Beaverbrook

171

at once saw the full implications of what his monarch had done: 'You have put your head on the execution block.' But as Mrs Simpson, according to the King, now 'preferred the morganatic marriage to any other solution,' Edward continued to insist it be considered. Later he was to admit 'I always thought I would get away with a morganatic marriage'. In fact the consensus of opinion both at home and in the Dominions was strongly against it. The Attorney-General highlighted its shortcomings in a brutal but vivid manner – the necessary legislation, he pointed out, would have to begin with words such as 'Whereas the wife of the king is queen, and whereas the present king desires to marry a woman unfit to be queen, be it enacted ...' The British Cabinet rejected the proposal outright.

Inexorably, as in some giant chess game, the King's freedom of manoeuvre was being reduced. Having formally brought the question of his marriage to the attention of the Government, only two choices now remained, abdication of the throne or abdication of Mrs Simpson. Delay was no longer possible. The protection afforded by the silence of the press was, as Hardinge had forecast, now lost. The unwitting instrument of this was Dr Blunt, the Bishop of Bradford, who at a diocesan conference expressed his hope that, as the Coronation approached, Edward would be more aware of his need for God's Grace, adding tetchily 'some of us wish that he gave more positive signs of his awareness'. Though the Bishop was not referring to Mrs Simpson but to irregular church attendance, his words started off an avalanche early in December. What concerned the King most in all the revelations was the sensational publicising of his lady friend, who in Britain, at least, had hitherto been protected by virtual anonymity. Millions of angry people, hearing of her for the first time, shared both Mrs Baldwin's feeling that 'Mrs Simpson has stolen the fairy prince' and Queen Mary's view that the country was being reduced to the level of Romania, where King Carol had caused havoc because of his relationship with Madame Lupescu.

The publicity so unnerved Mrs Simpson that, with the agreement of the King, she fled to the Continent. But both on her way through France, pursued by the press, and from her hideout at Cannes she pressed him not to give up the throne.

Do nothing rash, she advised, postpone the decision for a year. Similar advice was being given at the same time by Winston Churchill whom Edward, with Baldwin's permission, was consulting. By a strange irony, which Churchill as biographer of his great ancestor the Duke of Marlborough must have appreciated, the Churchill family began its rise to political power with John Churchill's intimate involvement with Charles II's mistress and his sister's attachment to James II. Now this last great Churchill's political career was put in jeopardy by his involvement in another King's intimate personal life. In this crisis, both his romantic attachment to the institution of monarchy and his warm personal regard for the King were deeply involved, and the sentimental statesman charged, like a knight errant, in the face of public opinion. At this stage in his career he was a political outcast from his Party and from government, following his ultra-conservative stand over India. More recently he had been seeking, with some success, to build up support in Parliament and the country for the need to rearm against Germany. At this juncture, his attempt to take the pressure off the King by pleading for delay in the House of Commons led to an outburst of fury against him. In Harold Nicolson's words: 'he has undone in five minutes the patient reconstruction work of two years.' Churchill himself momentarily felt his political career was finished. Never had his stock sunk so low; so low in fact that few credited him with the ability to rise again.

In contrast, Baldwin, who only a few weeks earlier had damaged his own reputation in his speech of 'appalling frankness' over rearmament, emerged from the crisis with his reputation fully restored. As Churchill in retrospect – after his own 'finest hour' – fully conceded, Baldwin on this occasion 'perceived and expressed the profound will of the nation'. On a more mundane level, Noel Coward is said to have put the royal champion in his place, when Churchill asked 'Why shouldn't the King marry his cutie?', by replying 'Because England does not want a Queen Cutie'.

Regardless of pressure on the King for a deferment of the decision, delay was no longer possible, nor indeed, as far as the King was concerned, desirable. Some support in the country, dubbed 'the King's Party', appeared to be building up but, according to Walter Elliot, the King discerned that the wish of such supporters was really to keep him with Mrs Simpson as his mistress, something he was still not prepared to entertain. On 5 December he cut the Gordian knot by formally informing his Prime Minister of his decision to abdicate.

Still Mrs Simpson in Cannes hoped that 'a way would be found out of the impasse' and over the telephone begged Edward not to take any irrevocable step. Up to this time she had comforted herself with the thought that 'they will never let him go'. When it became clear that he would go she decided that there was 'only one solution . . . to remove myself from the King's life'. She now publicly indicated her willingness 'to withdraw from a situation that has been rendered both unhappy and untenable'. Yet, according to Edward, when he told her over the telephone that 'the only conditions on which I can stay here are if I renounce you for all time . . . her answer to me was worthy of the occasion'. If this was so, what her offer to 'withdraw' was intended to mean is unclear, unless perhaps it indicated her willingness to give up any idea of marrying the King, having decided instead to return to him on some informal basis when the heat was off.

In any case, even if the King had accepted the withdrawal gesture, which he would not, it came too late. The formalities of the abdication were completed on 11 December. The Bill to give effect to it passed quickly through Parliament, and similar Bills passed through the Dominion Parliaments. The only hitch occurred when the Prime Minister of the Irish Free State, Eamon de Valera, at first declined to co-operate, in the happy expectation that if he did not King George VI could not succeed in Ireland. It was pointed out to him that in that case Edward VIII would continue to be King of Southern Ireland with Mrs Simpson as Queen Wallis. When he did take action de Valera used the opportunity to remove the monarchy for all practical purposes from the Irish constitution.

On the eve of his departure from Britain, Edward at last had his chance to broadcast his side of the story to the nation and the world. In a speech drafted by Monckton and embellished by Churchill he told his former subjects of his inability to continue as King 'without the help of the woman I love'. In bidding him farewell Churchill, with his sense of history, was moved to quote Marvell's famous lines on Charles I, 'He nothing common did nor mean upon that memorable scene', recalling the circumstances which had put Charles II into exile. Ironically, Charles II had returned home to enjoy a life filled with extra-marital pleasures, whereas this monarch, foreswearing mistresses, was going into what proved permanent exile to achieve satisfaction within marriage.

The final touch of irony was provided by another figure from the past, the old lady who, at the Ritz Hotel, pronounced on Edward's abdication speech. Alice Keppel, her mind as clear and incisive as ever, looked back into history at what she and her kind represented. With complete conviction she declared: 'Things were managed better in my day'.

Sources

A Little Pleasure Out Of The Way

page 17   **far outshining the Queen'**, Evelyn p. 520
               settling of her debts, Pepys VI, p. 92
page 18   **so great a gambler**, ibid, VII, p. 301
               laughing at his departure, Clarendon, **Continuation of His Life**, p. 438
               'held a sort of court', Burnet, p. 119
page 19   **over himself or his business'**, ibid, p. 62
               smitten by Castlemaine's looks, Pepys, II, pp. 64, 224
page 20   **all the tricks of Aretin that are to be practised to give pleasure'**, ibid, III, p. 115
               incapable of application to any that were not so', Hamilton, p. 105
               not the least notice is taken of their conduct', ibid, p. 189
page 21   **even on sacrament days'**, Burnet, p. 119
page 22   **the King would have it so'**, Evelyn, p. 674
               shall come into mighty favour', ibid, p. 786
               'But they, silly people! did not know her work', Pepys, VII, p. 83
               extravagant humours', Hamilton, p. 160
page 23   **by granting the last favours'**, ibid, p. 145
               bestow her favours upon Jacob Hall', ibid, p. 250
page 24   **not to revolt against Charles the Second'**, ibid, p. 217
               'dropped' a child at court while dancing, Pepys, III, p. 33
               into contact with Moll Davis and Nell Gwyn, Burnet, p. 178
page 26   **'a very familiar discourse'**, Evelyn, p. 552
               above sixty-thousand pounds', Burnet, p. 170
page 28   **lately introduced into their society'**, Hamilton, p. 250
page 29   **impeachment and imprisonment followed**, Harleian MSS, BM 7006, f. 171

Where The Deer Laid

page 32   after the manner of a married bride', Evelyn, p. 559
page 38   'all the world knows her storie', ibid, p. 628
           more than he himself had a mind to see', Burnet,
           Supplement, p. 135
page 39   excess of bravery could make them', Evelyn, p. 791
           it was a continual chiming', Bruce, Ailesbury Memoirs

The Forbidden Love Of Women

page 44   the most unguarded ogler of his time', Hamilton, p. 173
           a clap', Pepys, IV, p. 35
page 45   like a dog', ibid, V, p. 420; VI, p. 11
           and that he avoids', ibid, VI, p. 93
page 46   gradually wasting away', Hamilton, p. 274
page 48   his soul for a lot of trollops', Correspondence Complète de
           Madame Orleans, ed. M. G. Bruner, II, p. 94.
page 49   seduc'd by crafty knaves', Evelyn, p. 815
page 50   nor spake one word to the King', ibid, p. 839

But One Vice

page 54   'timely rescued', Sir John Reresby, Memoirs, p. 83
           has endeavoured to cover them', Burnet, Supplement, p. 190
page 57   squints like a dragon', Swift, Journal to Stella
           'the wisest woman I ever saw', Swift, Works, 2nd ed. III, p.
           47
page 60   to preach against that sin', Evelyn, p. 919
page 61   the thing is impossible', Private and Original
           Correspondence of Shrewsbury and William III, ed. W.
           Coxe, pp. 19–20.
           'such a good boy', Huygens, Journal, I, p. 401
           irregularity in his conduct', Burnet, IV, pp. 249–50
page 62   insinuations on that score', Huygens, Journal, II, p. 256
page 63   a more delightful spectacle', Selected Letters of Lady Mary
           Wortley Montagu, ed. Robert Halsband, p. 152

So Uncommon A Seraglio

page 66   who the true heir was in the family',
           A. Koecher, Die Princessen Von Ahlden, p. 225
page 67   the room where he was killed, Walpole, I,
           p. 313
page 68   the lower parts of her body . . .', Walpole, Reminiscences,
           ed. Paget Toynbee, p. 53

	she has captivated my son', Coxe, **Walpole**, I, p. 141
page 70	'with his left hand', Walpole, I, p. 314
page 72	an Irish peerage, Coxe, II, p. 59
	unpalatable policies, Diary of Mary Countess Cowper, p. 132
page 73	to the highest bidder, Coxe, I, p. 141
page 75	a faithful wife', Cowper, p. 98
	any such jewels abroad', ibid, p. 31
page 76	created a Countess', Walpole, III, p. 315
page 77	the utmost care of it', ibid

The Right Sow By The Ear

page 78	where it does not use to stand', Hervey, p. 278
	worthy to buckle her shoe', Coxe, II, p. 503
page 79	and addition to his pleasure', Hervey, pp. 41–2
page 80	'yes, my dear Howard, I am sure you will', ibid, p. 474
	you love to hide the Queen's', Walpole, I, p. 445
	doing it tomorrow', Coxe, II, p.4
page 81	till the clock struck', Walpole, I, p. 447
	'not to read any romances', Hervey, p. 472
	little dabs of money, ibid
	bending his will to hers', ibid, pp. 68–9
	sweeten the acid of the King's', ibid, p. 695
page 82	to whoever is proper', Suffolk, Letters, I, pp. 102, 245
page 83	opportunity of getting rid of her?', Hervey, p. 601
	dangerous sway of some new favourite', ibid, p. 383
page 84	his cuckold', ibid, p. 745
	a false heart', ibid, p. 491
page 85	who got it?', ibid, p. 744
	'a little in decline', ibid, p. 559
page 86	a much greater proof of his economy than his passion', ibid, p. 458
page 87	going to the close stool', HMC Egmont Diary, II, p. 209
	he wished to leave them', Hervey, p. 539
page 88	advice what she should do', ibid, pp. 745, 747
page 89	he had ever been acquainted with', ibid, p. 909
	the best interest in him', ibid, pp. 918 ff
page 91	I have no chance of succeeding', Coxe, II, pp. 4–5
	cost him a penny, HMC Egmont Diary
page 92	ces deux hommes là!' Walpole, II, pp. 252–3
	what he is often upon', Newcastle MSS
	sympathetic manner, Walpole, II, p. 259
page 93	opened it again', Newcastle MSS
	than he acts', HMC Egmont Diary

page 94   'easy in regard to amours', HMC Carlisle MSS Part VI, p. 167
           strong-box said to contain £10,000, Walpole, II, p. 305

Ye Pleasures of Elyssium

page 96   infernal cause Robinson', Aspinall, **Correspondence**, I, p. 56
           uncommonly grumpy', ibid, p. 73
page 97   'divinely pretty', ibid, p. 66
           would run off with her that night', ibid, p. 68
page 100   having solemnised', Holland, **Memoirs**, III, p. 19
page 101   an honourable one, Aspinall, III, pp. 173, 184
           to decide me to marriage', ibid, III, p. 169
page 103   'extreme intimacy', Hinde, pp. 87–8
page 104   cool herself in the rain', Lieven, p. 51
page 105   happiest of her connection with the Prince', Aspinall, III,
           p. 186
           a legacy of £30,000', ibid, VIII, p. 483

A Colt Out To Grass

page 107   rejoiced to see you', Aspinall, VIII, p. 404
           so long ignorant', ibid, VI, p. 221
           'to live with him publicly', **Granville Leveson-Gower
           Correspondence**, ed. Lord Granville, II, p. 298
           too familiar with her', Aspinall, VI, p. 353
page 108   first placed me', A. Leslie, **Mrs Fitzherbert**, II, p. 139
page 111   'a luxurious abundance of flesh', Lieven, p. 28
           ashamed of being so boyish', Letters of Lady Palmerston,
           p. 195
page 112   enormous balcony to wear them on', Lieven, p. 116
           fairy's boudoir', ibid, p. 182
           a great deal of harm', ibid, p. 23
           it will be too late', ibid, p. 227
page 113   'Heaven made us for one another', ibid, p. 305
page 114   rules him in the first place', ibid, p. 152
page 115   to attack Lady C', Elizabeth Longford, **Wellington, Pillar of
           State**, p. 183
page 116   an attack of prudishness', Lieven, p. 136
           it would not be for long', ibid, p. 145
           emerald on her arm', ibid, p. 229
           a habit he must have', ibid, p. 71

Those Damned Women

page 120   more uneasiness than enough', Aspinall, **Correspondence**, I,
           p. 324

page 120   fit to be touched with the tongs', ibid, II, p. 73
page 121   the appellation of the prodigal son', ibid, I, p. 336
            very unpleasant and of no use', ibid, I, p. 329
            What do you think, Madam?', F. Bickley, Diaries of Lord
            Glenbervie, I, p. 71
page 122   on my success', Aspinall, Correspondence, II, p. 208
page 124   offered assistance, ibid, VIII, p. 291
page 125   'bourgeois vulgarity', ibid, VI, p. 217
page 130   a dinner party there the same evening, The Holland House
            Diaries, ed. A. D. Kreiger,
            p. 362
page 131   unpleasant inmate', ibid, p. 370

Yielding To Temptation

page 133   early marriage for their son was imperative, see Roger
            Fulford, Dearest Child and Dearest Mama
page 134   Nellie Clifden, Magnus, pp. 47 ff.
page 135   the intended bridegroom had lost his innocence, ibid, p. 57
page 137   Hortense Schneider, ibid, p. 99
page 138   whose brother tried later (and unsuccessfully) to blackmail
            him, St Aubyn, pp. 151 ff
            carried on rather less discreetly, Brook - Shepherd, p. 67
page 139   another George IV as Prince of Wales', Magnus, p. 128
page 141   had a child by him, St Aubyn, pp. 155 ff
            to sort the matter out, R. Blake, Disraeli,
            pp. 692 ff
page.142   one more object of the Prince's attentions, Magnus, p. 190
            Miss Chamberlayne, Brook-Shepherd,
            pp. 134–5

Sinning As With A Cart-rope

page 145   friendship I had repudiated', Hibbert, Edward VII, p. 161
page 146   to distress Lady Charles, Magnus, p. 235
page 148   a sprig of parsley, Hibbert, p. 235 ff
            platonic for some years', Lang, My Darling Daisy, p. 81
page 149   their main dowry', Keppel, Edwardian Daughter, p. 7
page 152   to cultivate the King's friend, Brook - Shepherd, p. 141
            loyalty and discretion', Magnus, p. 260
page 153   a periodic guest at 10 Downing Street,
            R. Jenkins, Asquith 'La Favourita Keppel', Brook- Shepherd,
            p. 142
page 154   to have the honour of sleeping with the King', Ponsonby,
            p. 231
            semi-déclassé ladies and men to match',
            J. Wilson, Campbell-Bannerman, p. 143

page 155 **quite the same again'**, Keppel, p. 54
        at least for me', Brook-Shepherd, p. 359
page 155 **loved the more for it'**, A. J. Marder, **Fear God and Dread Nought** II, p. 42

The Tide Of His Ardour

page 158 **lots of girls before me'**, Martin, p. 12
        indulged in light-hearted fancy', Donaldson, p. 169
page 159 **went their separate ways sub rosa'**, Birkenhead, p. 126
        most fascinating aviator', Duchess of Windsor, p. 59
page 160 **depth of his devotion to her'**, Birkenhead, p. 125
        the talk of London', Chips Channon, **Diaries**, p. 77
        a new and glittering world', Duchess of Windsor, p. 201
page 161 **wholly American outlook'**, ibid, p. 190
        and I understood', Martin, p. 12
        friendship and love', Duchess of Windsor, p. 197
        'premonitory shiver', ibid, p. 216

Make Mrs Simpson His Mistress

page 164 **'let in some fresh air'**, Duke of Windsor, p. 280
        was to be his own', Birkenhead, p. 127
page 165 **the Simpsons' marriage'**, Donaldson, p. 209
page 166 **'Mr Simpson was a safeguard'**, ibid, p. 210
        new emotional centre for his life', Duchess of Windsor, p. 222
        plans would probably be frustrated', Donaldson, p. 245
page 167 **at this delicate juncture'**, Duchess of Windsor, p. 242
page 169 **I am prepared to go'**, Duke of Windsor, p. 329
        he should marry her', Donaldson, p. 302
        moral example to his people, Martin, p. 302
page 170 **notable precedents'**, Duke of Windsor, p. 332
        if it would interest her', Donaldson, pp. 282–3
        and I will', ibid. p. 302
        he was a mule', Martin, p. 12
page 173 **the patient reconstruction work of two years'**, Nicolson, **Diaries and Letters**, p. 284
        'the King's Party', C. Coote, **Companion of Honour**
page 174 **from the King's life'**, Duchess of Windsor, p. 259
        worthy of the occasion', Duke of Windsor, p. 405
page 175 **Charles II into exile**, Donaldson, p. 293

Select Bibliography

Andrews, Allen, *The Royal Whore*, Hutchinson, 1971

Ashley, Maurice, *Charles II*, Weidenfeld & Nicolson, 1971

Aspinall, A. (ed.), *Correspondence of George Prince of Wales*, Cassell & Co., 1963–71

Aspinall, A., *Mrs Jordan and Her Family*, Arthur Barker, 1951

Battiscombe, Georgina, *Queen Alexandra*, Constable, 1969

Baxter, Stephen B., *William III*, Longman, 1966

Beaton, Sir Cecil, *The Wandering Years*, Weidenfeld & Nicolson, 1969

Bevan, Bryan, *Charles the Second's French Mistress*, Robert Hale & Co., 1972

Birkenhead, Earl of, *Walter Monckton*, Weidenfeld & Nicolson, 1969

Blake, Robert, *Disraeli*, Eyre & Spottiswoode, 1966

Brook-Shepherd, Gordon, *Uncle of Europe*, Collins, 1975

Burnet, Gilbert, *History of My Own Time*, William Smith, 1835

    Supplement to Gilbert Burnet, History of My Own Time, ed. H. C. Foxcroft, Clarendon Press, 1902

Chapman, Hester W., *Mary II Queen of England*, Jonathan Cape, 1955

Chenevix Trench, Charles, *George II*, Allen Lane, 1973

Coxe, W., *Memoirs of Sir Robert Walpole*, T. Cadell & W. Davies, 1798

Croker, J. W. (ed.), *Letters of Henrietta Howard, Countess of Suffolk*, John Murray, 1824

Dickinson, H. T., *Bolingbroke*, Constable, 1970

Donaldson, Frances, *Edward VIII*, Weidenfeld & Nicolson, 1974

Evelyn, John, *Diary*, Oxford University Press, 1955

Forneron, H., *Louise de Keroualle, Duchess of Portsmouth*, Sonnenschein & Co., 1887

Gerson, N. B., *Lillie Langtry*, Robert Hale & Co., 1971

Hamilton, Anthony, *Memoirs of the Court of Charles II by Count Gramont*, George Bell & Sons, 1908

Hamilton, Elizabeth, *William and Mary*, Hamish Hamilton, 1972

Hartmann, C. H., *La Belle Stuart*, G. Routledge & Sons, 1926

    The Vagabond Duchess, G. Routledge & Sons, 1926

Haswell, Jock, *James II*, Hamish Hamilton, 1972

BIBLIOGRAPHY

Hatton, Ragnhild, *George I, Elector and King*, Thames & Hudson, 1979
Helsbrand, Robert (ed.), *Complete Letters of Lady Mary Wortley Montagu*,
    Oxford University Press, 1967
Hervey, Lord John, ed. Romney Sedgwick. *Some Materials towards Memoirs*
    of the Reign of King George II, Eyre & Spottiswoode, 1931
Hibbert, Christopher, *George IV, Prince of Wales*, Allen Lane, 1972
    George IV, Regent and King, Allen Lane, 1976
    Edward VII, Allen Lane, 1976
Hinde, Wendy, *George Canning*, Collins, 1973
Jordan, Ruth, *Sophie Dorothea*, Constable, 1971
Keppel, Sonia, *Edwardian Daughter*, Hamish Hamilton, 1958
Kreiger, A. D., *The Holland House Diaries*, Routledge & Kegan Paul, 1977
Lang, Theo, *My Darling Daisy*, Michael Joseph, 1966
Magnus, Philip, *Edward the Seventh*, John Murray, 1964
Martin, Gilbert, *Winston S. Churchill*, Vol. IV, Heinemann, 1976
Martin, Ralph J., *The Woman He Loved*, W. H. Allen, 1974
Melville, Lewis, *Lady Suffolk and Her Circle*, Hutchinson, 1924
Michael, Wolfgang, *England Under George I – The Beginnings*, Macmillan,
    1936
    England Under George I – The Quadruple Alliance, Macmillan, 1939
Ogg, David, *England in the Reign of Charles II*, Oxford University Press,
    1934
Pepys, Samuel, *Diary*, Bell, 1946
Plumb, J. H., *Sir Robert Walpole*, Vol. I, Allen Lane The Penguin Press,
    1956
    Sir Robert Walpole, Vol. II, Allen Lane The Penguin Press, 1960
Ponsonby, Sir Frederick, *Recollections of Three Reigns*, Eyre &
    Spottiswoode, 1951
Quennell, Peter (ed.), *The Private Letters of Princess Lieven to Prince*
    Metternich, 1820–1826, John Murray, 1937
Reresby, Sir John, *Memoirs*, Jackson Son & Co., 1936
St Aubyn, Giles, *Edward VII, Prince and King*, Collins, 1979
Scott, George, *Lucy Walters, Wife or Mistress*, Harrap, 1947
Sola Pinto, V. de, *Sir Charles Sedley*, Constable, 1927
Somerville, D.H., *King of Hearts*, George Allen & Unwin, 1962
Vanderbilt, Gloria, and Thelma Lady Furness, *Double Exposure*, Muller,
    1959
Van der Zee, Henri and Barbara, *William and Mary*, Macmillan, 1973
Walpole, Horace, *Memoirs of the Reign of George II*, Henry Colburn, 1846
Windsor, Duchess of, *The Heart Has Its Reasons*, Michael Joseph, 1956
Windsor, Duke of, *A King's Story*, Cassell & Co., 1951

Index

Abdul Karim ('the Munshi'), 152
Adelaide, Queen, 126–7, 128–9,
130
Albemarle, 1st Earl of, 54, 61, 149
Albert, Prince Consort, 132–5
Albert Victor, Prince, 136, 147
Alexander I, Emperor of Russia,
125
Alexandra, Queen, 129, 133–4,
135–6, 137–8, 141, 142, 143, 147,
148, 150–1, 154–5, 160, 169
Alington, 1st Baron, 152
Aly Khan, Prince, 160
Amelia ('Emily'), Princess, 83–4,
89
Anne, Queen, 43, 54, 55, 56, 57,
60, 64–5, 73, 79
Anne of Cleves, 16
Apsley, Frances, 55
Arlington, 1st Earl of, 18, 22, 31, 32
Asquith, H.H., 153, 154
Augusta, Princess of Wales, 93, 94
Aylesford, 7th Earl of, 141–2
Aylesford, Edith Countess of,
141–2

Bagehot, Walter, 137, 141
Baldwin, Stanley, 162, 165, 167,
168, 169, 170, 171, 173, 174
Baldwin, Mrs Stanley, 165, 172
Barlow, Mrs, see Walter, Lucy
Barucci, Giulia, 138, 148

Battenberg, Princess Alice of,
150–1
Battenberg, Prince Louis of, 143–4
Beaton, Cecil, 161
Beaverbrook, 1st Baron, 168, 171–2
Belasyse, Susan Lady, 46–7
Bellenden, Mary, 79
Beneni, Giulia, 148
Bentinck, Hans William, see
Portland, Earl of
Bentinck, William, 109
Beresford, Lord Charles, 144–6
Beresford, Lady Charles, 144–6
Berkeley, Sir Charles, 43
Berkeley, 5th Earl of, 125
Berkeley, Mary Countess of, 125
Bernhardt, Sarah, 142
Bernstorff, Baron, 71
Berwick, 1st Duke of, 46
Bessborough, Henrietta Countess
of, 107, 109
Blandford, Marquess of, 41
Blunt, Dr A.F., Bishop of
Bradford, 172
Bolingbroke, 1st Viscount, 65, 73,
74, 82, 83
Bolingbroke, Marie Viscountess, 73
Bolton, Henrietta Duchess of, 76
Boutourline, Comtesse de, 147–8
Brett, Anne, 76
Bristol, 2nd Earl of, 45
Brooke, Lord and Lady, see

Warwick, Earl and Countess of
Brougham, Henry, 108, 110
Buccleuch, Anne Countess of, 21
Buckhurst, Lord, 25
Buckingham, 1st Duke of, 56–7
Buckingham, 2nd Duke of, 23, 24, 26, 27, 31, 32
Buckinghamshire, Katherine Duchess of, 48
Burnet, Gilbert, Bishop of Salisbury, 13, 19, 21, 26, 27, 32, 43
Bute, 3rd Earl of, 94
Byron, 6th Baron, 109

Campbell, Mrs Patrick, 139
Campbell-Bannerman, Sir Henry, 154
Canning, George, 103, 107, 113, 114–15
Carnegie, Lord, 44
Carnegie, Anne Lady, 44
Carol, King of Romania, 172
Caroline, Queen (wife of George II), 69, 74, 78, 80–9, 91, 93
Caroline, Princess (daughter of George II), 84, 88
Caroline, Queen (wife of George IV), 102–4, 109–11, 121
Carrington, 1st Earl of, 138
Carteret, 2nd Baron, 74, 75–6
Cassel, Ernest, 151, 154
Castlemaine, 1st Earl of, 14
Castlemaine, Barbara Countess of, see Cleveland, Duchess of
Castlereagh, Viscount, 108, 113, 114
Catherine, Queen, 15, 16, 17, 20, 31, 32, 39, 44, 45
Catherine of Aragon, 165
Chamberlayne, Miss, 142, 147
Chandos, 1st Duke of, 25
Channon, Chips, 160
Charles I, 11, 12, 20, 24, 41, 174–5
Charles II, 11–40, 41, 42, 45, 48, 49, 53, 54, 55, 64, 73, 94, 102, 127, 128, 173, 175
Charles XV of Sweden, 137
Charlotte, Queen, 94, 95, 97, 102, 132

Chesterfield, 2nd Earl of, 14, 44
Chesterfield, 4th Earl of, 68–9, 72, 74, 92
Churchill, Arabella, 45–7, 49
Churchill, Jenny, 142
Churchill, John, see Marlborough, 1st Duke of
Churchill, Lord Randolph, 141–2
Churchill, Winston, 142, 153, 166, 173, 174–5
Cibber, Colley, 27
Clarendon, 1st Earl of, 15, 16, 18, 19, 21, 42, 43, 45
Clarke, Mary Anne, 108
Cleveland, Barbara, Duchess of, 13–24, 28–9, 31, 32, 33, 35, 39, 45, 57, 102
Clifden, Nellie, 134–5
Coke, Lady, 157
Colyear, Sir David, 52
Conyngham, 1st Marquess, 113
Conyngham, Elizabeth Marchioness, 111–16
Conyngham, 2nd Marquess, 139
Covell, Dr John, 58
Coventry, Sir John, 26
Coward, Noel, 173
Cowper, Mary Countess, 76
Cowper, Emily Countess, 111
Crew, Sir Thomas, 20
Crouch, Anna Maria, 100–1
Cumberland, Duke of (son of George II), 84
Cumberland, Duke of (brother of George III), 98
Curzon of Kedleston, 1st Marquess of, 52

Daly, Richard, 122
Danby, 1st Earl of, 22, 28, 33, 35
Darlington, Sophia Countess of, 67–8, 69, 70, 74–5, 76, 86
Darnley, Lady Katherine, see Buckinghamshire, Duchess of
Davis, Moll, 24–5
De L'Isle and Dudley, Sophia Lady, 126, 130
D'Elitz, Madame, 85, 93
Deloraine, Mary Countess of, 84,

85, 86–7, 88, 90
Denham, Lady, 45
Denmark, Princess Royal of, 125
Derwentwater, 2nd Earl of, 25
Derwentwater, 3rd Earl of, 73–4
De Valera, Eamon, 174
Disraeli, Benjamin, 141, 142
Donaldson, Frances, 161
Dorchester, Catherine Countess of, 47–52, 64
Dover, 1st Baron, 23, 24
Downshire, Mary Marchioness of, 125
Dryden, John, 25
Dudley Ward, Mrs, 157–8, 160

Edward IV, 170
Edward VII, 132–55, 156, 158
Edward VIII, 80, 156–75
Egremont, 3rd Earl of, 96, 126, 128
Elizabeth I, 17
Elizabeth II, 162
Elliot, Walter, 173–4
Emily, Princess, see Amelia, Princess
Erroll, Elizabeth Countess of, 126
Esher, 2nd Viscount, 151, 158
Evelyn, John, 12, 13, 17, 18, 20, 22, 26, 31, 32, 34, 38, 39, 45, 49, 50, 59, 60

Falkland, Amelia Viscountess, 158–9, 160
Falmouth, Mary Countess of, 44
Finch, Polly, 121–2
Fisher, Sir John, 146, 155
FitzClarence, Augustus, 128
FitzClarence, Frederick, 128
FitzClarence, George, see Munster, 1st Earl of
Fitzherbert, Maria, 99–101, 104–5, 107–8, 116–17, 120, 158
FitzJames, James, see Berwick, 1st Duke of
Ford, Sir Richard, 122, 124
Fortescue, Julia, 119
Fox, Henry, 92
Fox, Charles, 98, 100, 103
Frederick Prince of Wales, 85, 87,

93–4
Furness, Thelma Viscountess, 158–9, 160

George I, 64–77, 81, 82, 85, 171
George II, 69, 74, 78–93
George III, 93, 94, 95, 96, 97, 98, 101–2, 107, 109, 118, 119, 120–1, 122, 132
George IV, 95–117, 118, 120, 121, 124, 125, 133, 139, 148, 158
George V, 149, 151, 156–7, 159, 161–2, 164
George VI, 162, 174
George, Prince of Denmark, 54, 64
Gisors, Comte de, 91
Gladstone, W.E., 140–1, 143
Gloucester, Duke of (brother of George III), 125
Godfrey, Colonel Charles, 47
Gordon-Cumming, Sir William, 145
Grafton, 1st Duke of, 21–2
Grahame, Colonel James, 48
Gramont, Duc de, 148
Greville, Charles, 127, 129
Grey, 2nd Earl, 108, 128
Gwyn, Nell, 24, 25–8, 31, 34, 35, 37, 39, 40, 122

Hall, Jacob, 23–4
Hamilton, Anthony, 20, 23, 44, 45, 48
Hamilton, Lord George, see Orkney, Earl of
Hamilton, Mary, 96
Hardenburg, Count, 97
Hardenburg, Countess, 97
Hardinge, Alexander, 167, 168–9, 170, 172
Hardinge of Penshurst, 1st Baron, 150, 152, 153
Harley, Robert, 65
Harmsworth, Esmond, 171
Harris, Frank, 149
Hart, Charles, 25
Hartington, Marquess of, 139
Hazlitt, William, 122
Henrietta Maria, Queen, 11, 12, 21, 41

Henriette, *see* Orleans, Duchess of
Henri IV of France, 12, 51
Henry VIII, 14, 16, 165
Hertford, 5th Marquess of, 106–7, 112
Hertford, Isabella Marchioness of, 106–8, 111, 112, 113
Hervey, Lord, 76, 79, 80, 81, 82, 83, 84, 85, 86, 88, 89, 90, 93
Hervey, Lady, 76
Hibbert, Christopher, 147
Holland, 3rd Baron, 108, 126, 131
Howard, Henrietta, *see* Sussex, Countess of
Howe, 2nd Earl, 129
Hunt, Leigh, 108
Hyde, Anne, *see* York, Duchess of
Hyde, Edward, *see* Clarendon, Earl of

Irving, Washington, 127

James I, 56–7
James II, 11, 13, 16, 36, 39, 40, 41–52, 54, 55, 56, 58, 59, 60, 61, 64, 173
James, Henry, 151
Jennings, Sarah, *see* Marlborough, Duchess of
Jermyn, Henry *see* Dover, 1st Baron
Jersey, 4th Earl of, 101
Jersey, Frances Countess of, 101, 102–3, 104
Jordan, Mrs Dorothea, 122–4, 125

Kauchine, Mme, 147
Kendal, Ehrengard Duchess of, 68–77, 85, 171
Kennedy, Buttercup, 166
Kent, Duchess of (mother of Queen Victoria), 130, 131
Kent, Duke of (son of George V), 161
Keppel, Alice, 149–55, 156, 157, 158, 168, 175
Keppel, George, 149–50, 155, 169
Keppel, Joost van, *see* Albemarle, Earl of
Keroualle, Louise de, *see*
Portsmouth, Duchess of
Keyser, Alice, 153
Kielmannsegg, Baron von, 67, 75
Kielmannsegg, Baroness, *see* Darlington, Countess of
Killigrew, Elizabeth, 13
Kirke, Mary, 44
Knighton, Sir William, 114, 115
Konigsmarck, Count Phillip, 66–7

La Goulue, 148
Langtry, Lillie, 142, 143–4, 149
Le Breton, Dean, 143
Lennox, Lady Sarah, 94
Leopold, Prince, later King of the Belgians, 130
Leopold, Prince (son of Queen Victoria), 144
Lewis, Rosa, 138, 149
Lichfield, Charlotte Countess of, 39
Lieven, Princess, 104, 108, 111, 112, 113–14, 115–16
Lightfoot, Hannah, 94
Lindsay, Lady Charlotte, 125
Lingsingen, Caroline von, 120
Liverpool, 2nd Earl of, 112, 113, 114–15
Lloyd George, David, 152, 157
Louis XIV, 14, 30, 31, 35, 36, 40, 41–2, 46, 49, 53, 59, 70
Louis XV, 90, 91
Louis, Monsieur (son of George II), 87
Longueville, Duc de, 42
Lupescu, Madame, 172

Macclesfield, Anne Countess of, 76
Mahomet (servant of George I), 69
Maintenon, Madame de, 38, 49, 70, 73
Manchester, Louisa Duchess of, 139
Manzini, Hortense, *see* Mazarin, Duchesse de
Marlborough, 1st Duke of, 24, 46, 60, 65, 173
Marlborough, Sarah Duchess of, 7, 48, 59, 60, 64–5, 82
Marlborough 7th Duke of, 142

Martin, Sir Henry, 120
Martin, Ralph, 170
Martin, Sarah, 120
Marvell, Andrew, 11, 174–5
Mary II, 35, 43, 50, 51, 55–62
Mary, Queen (consort of George V), 151, 156, 161, 169, 172
Mary Beatrice, Queen, 47, 48, 50, 56
Masham, Abigail Lady, 65
Mazarin, Cardinal, 38
Mazarin, Duchesse de, 38, 39
Melbourne, Elizabeth Viscountess, 97
Melbourne, 2nd Viscount, 97, 139
Mercer Elphinstone, Miss, 125
Metternich, Prince, 113
Middleton, Catherine Countess of, 20
Millais, Sir John, 143
Monaco, Prince of, 38
Monckton, Walter, 159, 160, 161, 164, 166, 170, 174
Monmouth, 1st Duke of, 12, 21, 27, 39, 44, 49, 84
Montagu, Edwin, 129
Montagu, Lady Mary Wortley, 62, 72, 82
Montagu, Ralph, 28
Montespan, Madame de, 49
Mordaunt, Lady, 140
Mountbatten of Burma, 1st Earl, 144
Munster, Duchess of, see Kendal, Duchess of
Munster, 1st Earl of, 126, 127, 128, 129, 130, 131
Mustapha (servant of George I), 69

Napoleon I, Emperor, 97, 106, 111
Nelson, 1st Vicount, 119
Newcastle, 1st Duke of, 89, 92, 93
Nicolson, Harold, 150, 173
Norfolk, 11th Duke of, 22

Oldenburg, Grand Duchess of, 125
Orange, Mary Princess of, see Mary II
Orkney, Earl of, 62

Orkney, Elizabeth Countess of, 56–63, 64
Orleans, Henriette Duchess of, 30, 31
Orleans, Liselotte Duchess of, 66
Orleans, Philip Duke of ('Monsieur'), 30
Orleans, Philip Duke of (Regent Orleans), 40, 68, 76, 86

Palmer, Barbara, see Cleveland Duchess of
Palmer, Roger, see Castlemaine, Earl of
Palmerston, 3rd Viscount, 139
Pankhurst, Mrs Emmeline, 153
Pearl, Cora, 148
Peel, Sir Robert, 113, 129
Pegge, Catherine, 13
Pelham, Henry, 91–2
Pembroke, Elizabeth Countess of, 94
Pepys, Samuel, 17, 19, 22, 43, 45
Pergami, Bartolommeo, 109–10
Pitt, William (the Elder), 92
Platen, Countess, 67
Platen, Countess (daughter-in-law of above), 67, 75–6, 86
Pless, Daisy Princess of, 150
Plymouth, 1st Earl of, 13, 22
Pompadour, Madame de, 90, 91, 113
Ponsonby, Frederick, 154
Ponsonby, 2nd Baron, 114
Pope, Alexander, 82
Portland, Earl of, 54, 57, 59, 61
Portsmouth, Louise Duchess of, 30–40, 50, 56, 70, 94
Pourtales, Comtesse Edmond de, 147
Price, Goditha, 44, 45

Raffray, Mary Kirk, 166
Richmond, 1st Duke of, 36
Robinson, Mary ('Perdita'), 96, 122
Rochester, 2nd Earl of, 26
Rochester, 4th Earl of, 50
Rosebery, 5th Earl of, 138
Rothermere, 1st Viscount, 171

Rothschild, Baronne Alphonse de, 147

Sagan, Princesse de, 138, 147
St Albans, 1st Duke of, 26, 28, 40
Salisbury, 3rd Marquess of, 145–6
Sandwich, 1st Earl of, 22
Schneider, Hortense, 137–8
Schulenburg, Ehrengard Melusine von der, see Kendal, Duchess of
Sedley, Catherine see Dorchester, Countess of
Sedley, Sir Charles, 48, 51
Sevigné, Madame de, 34
Shaftesbury, 1st Earl of, 36, 37
Shakespeare, William, 25
Shelton, Sir Bevil, 58
Shrewsbury, 15th Earl of, 60–1
Shrewsbury, Adelaide Duchess of, 76
Simpson, Ernest, 159–60, 165, 166, 169
Simpson, Wallis, 70, 155–74
Sophia Dorothea (wife of George I), 65–7, 68, 76
Southampton, 1st Duke of, 14, 21
Stuart, Frances, 19, 22–3, 28
Suffolk, 9th Earl of, 80, 84
Suffolk, Henrietta Countess of, 79–83, 88
Sunderland, 4th Earl of, 72
Sundon, Charlotte Lady, 82
Sussex, Anne Countess of, 14, 39
Sussex, 1st Duke of, 131
Swift, Jonathan, 57, 73, 82

Tankerville, Camilla Countess of, 84
Townshend, 2nd Viscount, 71–2, 74, 75
Tudor, Lady Mary, 25
Turenne, Marshal Henri, 41
Tylney-Long, Catherine, 124

Vane, Anne, 93
Vane Tempest, Lady Susan, 141
Vendôme, Philippe de, 38
Verneuil, Dame, 147
Victoria, Queen, 118, 130, 131, 132–7, 139, 140–1, 144, 151, 152, 162
Villiers, Elizabeth, see Orkney, Countess of
Villiers, Lady Frances, 57
Villiers, George, see Buckingham, 1st Duke of

Walmoden, Amelia Sophia von, see Yarmouth, Countess of
Walpole, Horace, 70, 76, 77, 79, 81, 83, 91, 93
Walpole, Sir Robert, 71–6, 79, 81–91
Walsingham, Petronille Countess of, 70–1, 73
Walter, Lucy, 12, 13, 21, 37, 49
Walters, Catherine, 148
Warwick, 5th Earl of, 144, 146, 149–50
Warwick, Daisy Countess of, 144–7, 148–9, 151, 152
Washington, George, 118
Wauchope, Captain, 57
Wellesley-Pole, William, 124
Wells, Winifred, 24, 28
Wellington, 1st Duke of, 96, 110, 115, 116, 124
William III, 35, 37, 42, 50, 51, 52, 53–62, 64, 69, 149
William IV, 118–131, 132
William the Silent, 53
William II, Emperor of Germany, 152
Winne, Sally, 120
Woodville, Elizabeth, 170
Wright, Alderman, 26
Wycherley, William, 23
Wyckham, Miss, 125
Wyndham, William, 84, 85

Yarmouth, Amelia Countess of, 85–93, 94
York, Anne Duchess of (wife of James II), 42–3, 44, 45, 46
York, Frederick, Duke of (son of George III), 97, 108